Praise for
Little House on the Freeway

"The Bible says to be still and know God—a challenge in our harried culture. This book will help you achieve relational wellness with God, your spouse, and your children."

—DON M. "BUBBA" CATHY, sr. vice president of Chick-fil-A Inc.

"Like learning to breathe, blink, or swallow, we assume we'll automatically know how to rest. But in the rush of today's world, what was once an automatic response is now an acquired behavior. Tim Kimmel teaches us how to rest…and, therefore, how to live."

—ELISA MORGAN, MOPS International

"*Hurry* and *busyness* are everyday parts of modern life. True priorities of things that matter most may be lost. *Little House on the Freeway* offers biblical insights and principles to our hurried existence—help from the Word of God for the life being lived in the fast lane."

—BILLY GRAHAM

"Once again, Tim Kimmel has stayed away from the typical mantras offered by 'family experts' and given us a fresh, relevant message for parents and families."

—CLIFF YOUNG, lead singer of Caedmon's Call

"*Little House on the Freeway* is a book that runs over all our excuses about life-bustling, driving home our need for balance and peace."

—PATSY CLAIRMONT, author of *God Uses Cracked Pots*

"If you're looking for an antidote to family stress and strain—look no further. For those who want to steer clear of unhealthy stress and toward family closeness, this book is 'must read' material."

—JOHN TRENT, PhD

"I am thrilled that Tim Kimmel is re-releasing this updated classic. *Little House on the Freeway* will profoundly impact your priorities for marriage and family and have an enduring influence on you and your legacy."

—Dr. Crawford W. Loritts Jr., senior pastor
of Fellowship Bible Church

"If you feel that your family's schedule is out of control and going way too fast, then you need Tim Kimmel's wisdom. If you feel that you're doing just fine, then you may desperately need this book."

—Steve Farrar, Point Man Leadership Ministries

"In a warm and at times humorous style, Kimmel offers sound, practical counsel on how to restore calmness and rest to marriage, family life, workplace, and relationship with God."

—*Focus on the Family Magazine*

LITTLE
HOUSE
ON THE
FREEWAY

HELP FOR THE HURRIED HOME

OTHER BOOKS BY TIM KIMMEL

Grace-Based Parenting
Raising Kids for True Greatness
Home Grown Heroes
Why Christian Kids Rebel
The High Cost of High Control
Raising Kids Who Turn Out Right
Basic Training for a Few Good Men
Extreme Grandparenting

SMALL GROUP DVD STUDIES BY TIM KIMMEL

Grace-Based Parenting
Raising Kids for True Greatness
Raising Kids Who Turn Out Right
Basic Training for a Few Good Men
Extreme Grandparenting
The Hurried Family

LITTLE HOUSE ON THE FREEWAY

HELP FOR THE HURRIED HOME

TIM KIMMEL

Multnomah
BOOKS

LITTLE HOUSE ON THE FREEWAY
PUBLISHED BY MULTNOMAH BOOKS
12265 Oracle Boulevard, Suite 200
Colorado Springs, CO 80921

ISBN 978-1-59052-612-5

Library of Congress Cataloging-in-Publication Data
Kimmel, Tim.
    Little house on the freeway : help for the hurried home / Tim Kimmel.
        p. cm.
    Includes bibliographical references.
    ISBN 978-1-59052-612-5
    1. Christian life. 2. Marriage—Religious aspects—Christianity. 3. Family—Religious life. I. Title.
    BV4501.2.K4933 2008
    248.4—dc22

                              2008011922

Printed in the United States of America
2013

10 9 8 7 6 5 4 3

SPECIAL SALES
Most WaterBrook Multnomah books are available in special quantity discounts when purchased in bulk by corporations, organizations, and special interest groups. Custom imprinting or excerpting can also be done to fit special needs. For information, please e-mail SpecialMarkets@WaterBrookMultnomah.com or call 1-800-603-7051.

To Darcy,
who brings more calm and confidence to
a home than this man deserves.

CONTENTS

FOREWORD

When I was invited to write the original foreword to *Little House on the Freeway,* I thought it was best book I had ever read on the subject of dealing with the hurried lifestyle. It still is. Maybe that's why it was so quick to gain "classic" status and has remained in print the entire time.

But in the two decades since its first release, much has changed. Among other things, technology has added a long list of daily necessities that didn't even exist when Tim wrote the original version. And the war on terror now casts its frightening shadow over our daily lives. Hurried lives are no longer the exception in average homes; they're the rule.

If anything, the need for the principles in this book are more relevant now than when they were first written. That's why I'm so excited about this new updated version of Tim Kimmel's original work. The six necessities for rest that he gleaned for us from the Bible were urgently needed in the closing decade of the twentieth century. They make even more sense now. That's because they're timeless.

The good news is that you not only have the benefit of learning how to make these timeless principles part of your lifestyle, but you can learn them in a timely new way. I love how Tim has rewritten this book against the backdrop of new technologies, demanding economies, and a changing world context. I'm especially excited about his additional chapter, "Little House on the Internet."

Little House on the Freeway isn't about trying to retreat to a by-gone era but instead shows us how to face the hurried lifestyle head on…with calm and confidence. It's fresh air for the extended Smalley family that spends a lot of their time trying to catch their breath. And it's going to breathe some peace into your busy lives too. A past generation revered the original. The next generation is going to love this timely and time-less new version.

I invite you to turn the page and start gaining seasoned help for your hurried home.

—Gary Smalley
BRANSON, MISSOURI

PART

1

IN SEARCH OF
PEACE AND QUIET

Whatever happened to uncluttered and uncomplicated lives? Maybe every generation asks the same question. But not every generation has had to deal with pressures like ours. We've plunged headfirst into the twenty-first century, knowing that the future has arrived but not sure we're actually ready.

It seems like only yesterday our grandfathers were plowing the lower forty, walking to school, going to town once a week, and getting to bed by eight o'clock. Millions of people who made their debut on our planet in the early part of the twentieth century remember when their towns looked like a chapter from Laura Ingalls Wilder's classic *Little House on the Prairie*.

But Walnut Grove has changed a lot since they added the Taco Bell, Wal-Mart, and Starbucks. Quiet, simple lives have given way to off-ramps, ATMs, and Quarter Pounders with Cheese.

Pa Ingalls wouldn't believe his eyes.

Life will never again be like it was when people lived in their quiet little houses on the prairie. Jets slamming into the World Trade Center changed all of that for good. Besides, we all live too close to the freeway to back away from the hold it has on us. Together we enjoy all the benefits and conveniences of high-tech, high-speed living. And together we suffer the inevitable consequences.

The family that makes it through life without bearing the marks of a hurried home is the rare exception, not the rule.

It's like the *Peanuts* cartoon in which Lucy offers one of her unsolicited observations about life to Charlie Brown.

"Life," she muses, "is like a deck chair. Some place it so they can see where they are going. Some place it so they can see where they have been. And some place it so they can see where they are at present."

Charlie Brown replies, "I can't even get mine unfolded!"

Many of us feel as if we can't get our lives unfolded. With all the worry and hurry around us, it's difficult to gain any kind of honest perspective. Sometimes it takes a whack on the side of the head just to get our attention.

The Hurried Lifestyle: Marshall's Story

Marshall sat in his car outside the heart specialist's office, his forehead against his hands on top of the steering wheel. Tears filled his eyes and dripped in dark, wet circles onto his jeans.

The cardiologist's voice had been grim. He wasn't bluffing this time. "It's up to you, Marshall. Either slow down *immediately*, or put your affairs in order and say your good-byes. I can guarantee that if you don't back off the pace you're on, you won't live long enough to walk your daughter down the aisle. We've talked about this before, and I don't know how to warn you any more strongly. The amount of stress in your life is out of control. It's got to stop *now!*"

Marshall's hands gripped the wheel. *How can this be?* He had all the things that are supposed to make a person complete. He had a loving, devoted wife and three fairly normal kids. Life had dished him out a generous piece of the American pie. And in the spiritual category, he was a Christian and a well-respected leader in his church.

An overwhelming feeling of betrayal swept over him, bringing anger after the tears. For Marshall, the words *slow down* were about equal in dread to the death sentence his doctor had pronounced over him. And even with the doctor's warning ringing in his ears, cutting large pieces out of his schedule seemed flat wrong. Slow down? It was out of the question—even if he *wanted* to. His commitments to his clients, his partners, and his creditors would not allow him the luxury. He was hooked, frustrated, and tired...so tired.

How had he ever climbed onto such an accelerating treadmill? Days filled with responsibilities, nights filled with obligations, family relationships badgered by distractions, and meals choked down on the run. He knew he was bucking terrible odds by continuing his frenetic pace, but...well, he'd grown accustomed to his crazy life.

Like many of us, Marshall was in desperate need of genuine rest—yet was unwilling to ask the hard questions and make the difficult decisions involved in finding it.

The Hurried Lifestyle: Marsha's Story

Marsha was a nonstop woman. She was a busy wife and a hurried mother. Her home was equipped with the latest conveniences designed to do the mundane—so she could be freed up to do the all the stuff that kept her running at full speed. Her life was full speed to outsiders looking in, but everything about her internal systems seemed to indicate that *exhausted* would be a better word to sum up the state she was in.

Marsha was the only woman on her block with the "luxury" of staying home and focusing all her attention on raising her children. This meant that she had even more time than a "working" mother to jam in daily obligations to her children, her church, her kids' school, her in-laws, the country club, the baby-sitting co-op, and her former sorority.

Balancing the academic and social calendars of one preteen and two teenagers kept Marsha in her car most of the time, providing taxi service to school, lacrosse practice, band rehearsal, and swim team. Add in four pilates and one yoga workout a week, two women's Bible studies, volunteering at the hospital, and the ever-present demands of keeping a large house functioning at capacity, and you've got a woman who barely has time to change her mind, let alone her outfit. If the GPS on Marsha's car could speak its mind, it would tell her to stay home and take a nap.

Even though they didn't need the money, Marsha thought it made sense to add a growing eBay business to the open moments she had in her busy days. Marsha was T-I-R-E-D. Physically, emotionally, and spiritually, this hurried woman was in deep need of genuine rest.

In an effort to recapture this missing element in her world, Marsha took a daily one-hour vacation. At 2:00 p.m. every weekday, she would retire to her room, get comfortable on her bed, pick up the remote control, and push the appropriate button that called up channel forty-two on her cable menu. Then, for the next fifty-eight minutes, Marsha would join Laura Ingalls and her family as they experienced life in their little house on the prairie.

Marsha envied the pioneer family's seemingly uncomplicated lifestyle. She loved watching reruns of *Little House on the Prairie* on the TV Land network. Choices were fewer back then—and seemingly easier to make. The list of necessities for happiness consisted of little more than food, clothing, shelter, and love.

When did it all change? Marsha wondered as the lilting *Little House* theme signaled the end of yet another episode. *When did the list of necessities for happiness get so long? Somewhere between yesterday and tomorrow it's been expanded to include snowboards, laser eye surgery, pay-per-view TV, wireless Internet access, iPods, and breast implants. How did life get so complicated?*

Marsha's life was full to the point of overflowing, but she was running on empty when it came to inner contentment. Her spirit craved rest the way an exhausted body craves sleep. But she had no idea where to find it.

Rest Is (Not) Out of the Question

Marshall and Marsha are not alone, and they aren't without hope. In the midst of the most hurried and haggard schedules, they can discover lasting calm that reaches into the very center of their lives. And so can we.

God wants us to enjoy genuine rest—not just the "good night's sleep" kind of rest that satisfies the body but an internal rest that bathes the soul in contentment.

It's a relief to know that rest isn't out of the question. There are elements of rest that can be appropriated into our lives. In the pages that follow, we will look at the foundation for genuine rest along with six crucial battlegrounds where the struggle for rest can be waged and won.

But there is a paradox ahead. As we will see in later chapters, these very elements that bring us rest may also force us to redefine our comfort zones.

When a Paradox Becomes a Principle

I'm certain that a similar sense of paradox wasn't lost on Joshua as he stood poised to cross the Jordan River. Forty years of restless wandering were behind him. He and Caleb were the only survivors of the original gathering of pilgrims that had left Egypt four decades earlier. The decaying remains of that bickering and idolatrous generation lay lifeless under the Sinai sands.

Moses, his leader and close friend, had been the last to go. Now General Joshua, a fearless spy and decorated war hero, was commander in chief of Israel. Behind him stood the offspring of that "wilderness" group—women and children eager to stop wandering. Beside him stood thousands of untried armor-clad soldiers, anxious to get their first taste of battle. Before him sprawled the unconquered mountains and valleys of the Promised Land.

The assurance of God's own words washed across Joshua's spirit as he prepared his people to claim their promised real estate: "The LORD your God is giving you rest and has granted you this land" (Joshua 1:13).

Ahead of Joshua lay struggle and hardship; behind him, only death in the desert. Yet all was not lost. God had spoken a promise that must have brought incredible hope to the weary commander's heart. God had told him that as surely as he would enter the land, he would enter into rest as well.

The paradox is really a principle for us today: *genuine rest is never far away from the middle of a challenge.* Joshua's giants were Canaanite warriors who cast long and intimidating shadows. And just like them, the giants facing you and me cast intimidating shadows as well. What you'll find most ironic in all of this is that the secrets of genuine rest promised to the nation of Israel are still keys to living life to the fullest today.

Years ago, a contest was held in which artists were invited to paint a picture of peace. The entries were eventually narrowed down to just two. The first artist had interpreted perfect peace by painting a quiet lake cradled high in the lonely mountains. The second artist painted a thundering waterfall with the branch of a birch tree bending over the foam. On the fork of that limb, just shy of the spray, a robin sat undisturbed on her nest.

You and I can have that kind of peace. Our lifestyles are filled with unavoidable stress and activity that don't look like they're going to go away. In learning what God's Word has to say about genuine rest, we too can gain an unshakable calm. Even in the middle of the storm.

2

SEVEN MARKS OF A HURRIED FAMILY

Over the past fifteen years, I've watched the speed at which we live our lives shift from second gear into *overdrive*. But since few people these days have driven a stick shift, how about this analogy? We're running at mach 2 with our hair on fire.

While counseling individuals and couples over the past few decades, I've observed at least seven characteristics that mark hurried families. Separately, these characteristic are toxic. Combine them and they're deadly. They kill the faith, joy, and love needed for a family to stay calm and connected.

I'd like you to join me for a stroll down a street in a typical suburban American neighborhood. The houses are cloned by architects; the families, by a hurried culture.

We'll stop by seven homes for a closer look. As we peer through the windows, don't be too surprised if you catch a glimpse of your own family.

The Baileys: Can't Relax

Meet the Baileys…if you can. It's hard to get to know them because their schedule doesn't allow them much time to cultivate close friendships. But they do have a lot of acquaintances. They meet them through the numerous projects that make up their day.

Frank, a salesman, sets the pace. He's so used to a crowded schedule that he feels guilty when he isn't in motion. He belongs to two civic clubs (they're great for networking), oversees the United Way fund drive every year, coaches soccer, plays racquetball twice a week, trains for an annual marathon, teaches junior high Sunday school, and maintains a beautifully landscaped yard. His latest toy is a cell phone that also gives Frank constant access to his text messages, e-mail, family photo albums, and 40 gigs of rock and roll.

His wife, Leslie, works part-time. That way she has plenty of time left over to be busy. Leslie is always creating new projects. It's interesting to visit their house once a year to see all the changes she has made. "Redecorating is the way I relax," she says. Like her husband, Leslie is committed to physical fitness and civic improvements. She works out every day, publishes a blog on important political and social issues, and volunteers several hours a week with her political party. The only time her neighbors get to visit with her is when she knocks on their door with yet another petition.

The Bailey kids are busy being president of this and captain of that. They seldom have time to get in trouble. Most parents would love to have them as their children.

The Baileys are the envy of the neighborhood. On the surface they look ideal, but their industrious veneer hides one of the standard marks of a hurried family: *they can't relax.*

It's not that they *don't* relax; it's that they *can't,* even when they try. What some would describe as resourcefulness is just a cover-up for restlessness. It's their way of not having to be idle. Charles Swindoll capsulizes their dilemma:

Busyness rapes relationships. It substitutes shallow frenzy for deep friendship. It promises satisfying dreams, but delivers hollow nightmares. It feeds the ego, but starves the inner man. It fills the calendar, but fractures the family. It cultivates a program, but plows under priorities.[1]

The Baileys aren't bad. They're just too busy.

The Grahams: Can't Enjoy Quiet

You know when you're nearing the Grahams' residence because of the sounds blaring from behind their walls. It's hard to tell exactly what the music is, however, because of the way the various styles collide as they emanate from different rooms. The Grahams' house is a confluence of conflicting entertainment.

As you walk in the front door, you notice the television talking to itself in the family room. Nobody's watching it. The latest video game blasts from their thirteen-year-old's room while rap music keeps up its nonstop cadence from somewhere deep in their sixteen-year-old's bedroom. (It's the room farthest from the parents'.) Janet Graham is talking on the phone through a wireless headset while tossing a salad for tonight's dinner. From her vantage point in the kitchen, she keeps an eye on the HDTV blaring from the wall behind the dining room. Jerry Springer has just begun another tabloid interview: transvestites who were their own prom date!

Gordon Graham loves romantic jazz. You can usually hear Diana Krall before you can see Gordon's car. He likes to eat as soon as he arrives home. Tonight will be no exception. The family will gather in the dining room for supper. As usual, they will find out more about the lives of the characters on some reality TV show than their own.

Every Graham sleeps with his or her iPod on. Their bodies slumber, but their spirits do not rest. They're a sad example of the second mark of a hurried family: *they can't enjoy quiet.*

The Grahams are intimidated by silence. As their hearts cry out for rest, they answer back with entertainment. By keeping their brains occupied with external sights and sounds, they don't have to face the emptiness within. Noise is the Prozac that helps them cope with inner restlessness.

The greatest gift the Graham family could receive would be for lightning to strike a local substation and shut off the power for several days. But knowing Gordon Graham, he'd just crank up the Honda generator he keeps for just such "emergencies." He bought it last summer for their two-week camping trip. They almost couldn't get it in their SUV— what with the TV, DVD, and their laptops taking up so much room.

The Joneses: Never Satisfied

As we walk toward the end of the block, the noise from the Grahams' house is only a faint din in the distance. Turning to the right, you can't help being impressed by the two-story plantation-style house about halfway down the street. It's the largest and most beautifully manicured home in the community. That's the Joneses. You know them—they're the ones everyone is trying to keep up with.

Brian Jones is a professional landscaper. Sharon Jones is a professional shopper. She boasts that she graduated magna cum Visa. She also sells real estate. Both husband and wife enjoy the same hobbies—reading catalogs and shopping online. Sharon's best friends are her two daughters, Molly and Mindy. They spend most of the time working on their friendship at the mall, and they never come home empty-handed.

Michael, their youngest child, is preoccupied with upgrading. He is upgrading his bike, his computer, his skateboard, his image, and his friends. He's a chip off the new and improved block.

Michael's father buys a new car as soon as the latest models are showcased. He's had three boats in six years. He's the only guy in the neighborhood who had an addition built on to his pool. A garage sale at their house is like a blue-light special at Neiman Marcus.

The Joneses telegraph the third mark of a hurried family. But contrary to what you might think, it's not materialism. With the economic blessings the average American family enjoys, most homes today would be considered materialistic. The Jones family is badgered by a far more serious and subtle enemy: *the Joneses are never satisfied.* They aren't satisfied with what they have, where they are, or who they are.

For this family, contentment is always just around the corner—in the latest shipment from Buy.com, in being the first one on their block to have one. One *what*? It doesn't really matter as long as they're first. They are a family robbed of rest. They have failed to see that satisfaction is a choice.

The Gardners: An Absence of Absolutes

The somewhat predictable Joneses are a contrast to their neighbors, Steve and Millie Gardner. The only thing you can be certain of with the Gardners is their uncertainty. They display an overwhelming lack of permanence in their family, and they have a hard time imagining life beyond the moment.

Their home is a collection of unfinished projects, cluttered with unneeded items bought on impulse and often in dire need of repair. They are great at

- starting but poor at finishing
- pursuing ideas without a plan
- searching but never finding
- consistently confusing yes and no

They tried several churches. The Presbyterians were too formal. The Baptists were too narrow. The charismatics were too emotional. The Gardners enjoyed the fellowship and needed the leadership, but their vacillating standards have denied them a safe harbor in church. It's just a matter of time before someone gets close enough to the Gardners to see their inconsistencies. Running always seems to be the only tolerable option.

Both Steve and Millie have had lapses into infidelity. Steve has rationalized them as passing indulgences; Millie was getting even the first time…and just adding a little flavor to her routine existence the second time. Each marital betrayal has pushed them light-years apart.

Steve is being scrutinized by the IRS. They're sure that he keeps two sets of books. In time he, like all men with his problem, will get caught. People with shifting standards fail to see that the piper always gets paid.

Steve and Millie are a good example of the folly of situational ethics. They make up the rules as they go along. As far as they're concerned, God handed Moses the Ten Suggestions on Sinai, not the Ten Commandments. It has all backfired on them, though, and their children are the unfortunate wounded.

Take Jeremy, for instance. He's trying to graduate from high school. It has become a real challenge since he's a habitual cheater. He lacks basic skills and therefore lacks confidence. He copes by regularly getting high and watching Internet porn. His parents don't like it, but neither they nor he feels that they are qualified to criticize him.

His sixteen-year-old sister is an even sadder commentary on the wishy-washy Gardners. She developed early. Her father encouraged her to dress in a way that accented her figure. If he knew that his favorite poker buddy molested her when she was twelve, he'd kill him. She has big problems now. Two months ago she got pregnant. Her parents are demanding that she abort the baby, but she wants to keep the child and rear it herself.

It hurts to watch the restless, wandering Gardners. They refuse to recognize an absolute set of standards in their lives and therefore never feel sure of themselves. They go to church and occasionally read the Bible, but they aren't convicted by it enough to let it guide them in specific decisions. They are restless because they live for the immediate at the expense of the permanent.

Every neighborhood has a few Gardners living in it. You watch them take one insecure step after another through a daily maze and shake your head. I pity the Gardners. It's as if they're trying to navigate the open seas without a compass or a rudder. They're lost and confused, always pursued by a nagging sense of guilt. They need rest.

The Moores: Suffering Servants

As we leave the Gardners arguing in the background, we come to a family that is always engulfed in activity. That's the Moores.

The Moores live in every neighborhood. They're always there when you need them, quick to sympathize, ready to sacrifice.

When the church lost its Boy Scout leader, Mitchell Moore came to the rescue. When a family from Sunday school had their house gutted by fire, the Moores immediately took them in. If you need your car fixed, your house painted, your kids watched, you call the Moores. They have time to nurture everyone else's marriage and family life—except their own. Their marriage, their kids, and their spirits feel the neglect. Lately their bodies have been showing the neglect. Mitchell is quick to take time to meet you for breakfast to hear your problems but can never seem to find time to put a few miles on his running shoes.

They are great people who do wonderful things for others, but they're unhappy. Why? Because they're righteousness *addicts:* they do good things for wrong reasons. Their sympathetic gift is more often a cover-up for their own insecurities. It's also a noble way to keep from having to address their own inner problems.

And what might those problems be? They need approval. They need to hear compliments in order to convince themselves that they're valuable.

We all love the Moores. At some time or another, we all *need* the

Moores. But we don't want to *be* the Moores. Their struggle for approval makes us tired. They are marked as a hurried family because they don't know how to handle their insecurities. They are denied rest by their inordinate need to be liked.

The Newberrys: A Storm Beneath the Calm

We wave to Grace Moore as she pulls out of her driveway to take dinner to a couple from church who just had a baby. Directly across the street, the Newberrys' home is a welcome sight for our hurried eyes. Finally we've found a family who seems to have grasped the concept of rest.

As you get to know the Newberrys, you are impressed by the calm, controlled way they move through life. Most of what they do appears to be done with relative ease. It's reflected in the peace they exude.

Norma, in particular, comes across as one of the most "together" friends in her group. She never seems to be in a rush. Her car is usually moving a couple miles under the speed limit. Perhaps the best word to describe the way she has decorated her house is *tranquil*.

Beneath Norma's calm smile, however, she hides a little secret. Her smile masks a plaguing problem that she successfully shrouds from her family and friends. Norma Newberry is a confirmed, card-carrying worrier.

Different from the legitimate worries that accompany the basic question marks of life, Norma is constantly shadowed by irrational worry when encountering circumstances beyond her control. Sure, we all like to have as much control as possible over any given situation, but a healthy outlook recognizes that life serves up a vast menu of uncertainties. We are at the mercy of an assortment of variables.

That's not Norma's style. When she was a little girl, her daddy walked out on her and her mom. Her mother did her best to make the most of unfortunate circumstances, but the devastation to Norma's security system left her unsure of just about everything—especially herself. She compensated on the outside but never gained confidence on the inside. Her childhood trauma has haunted her throughout her life. It boils down to two gnawing frustrations: fear of loss and an inordinate desire for gain.

Daily she worries that her husband, Ken, will lose his job. Who cares that he has been secure in his position for over eighteen years? She's certain that one day he's going to come home carrying a cardboard box filled with personal belongings from his office.

She worries that her children are going to be in an accident. If they're late coming home from school or an appointment, she's ringing their cell phones. If they don't pick up, her first thought is to call the police and local hospital to check the accident report. She's actually done it a few times. When her son went to camp for the first time, she invented lame reasons to call him every day to make sure he wasn't upset or injured. She worries that her mother (who is in great health for her age) is going to suffer some kind of medical setback. She hordes her close friends and hates it when they develop new relationships, fearing that competitive friendships might turn them against her. Her worry never shows on the outside. It would be better if it did. It exists just beneath the surface—the storm beneath the calm.

Rest eludes the Newberry house because one member traffics in fear. They aren't a weak family, just fragile. Worry is a series of hairline fractures running through the foundation of their home. If everything goes well, they will endure, but that's one "if" they can't count on.

Their home is one you're excited to enter but can't wait to leave. Fear has such a choke hold on one person living there that everyone feels edgy. It's a shame. The Newberrys are such nice people.

The Evanses: World-Class Overachievers

We'll drop in on one more home on Hurried Street: the residence of Allen and Minya Evans. An all-American family, they fail to enjoy rest because they are overachievers. They are the by-product of a competitive society that seems to whistle and applaud only for winners.

Allen's love affair with winning started as a child. His father didn't have much time for him. He even hinted that Allen lacked the raw talent needed to be successful. Allen countered by excelling in school, Little League, and student government. He was pleased to see his father's unabashed approval. Once he realized what it took to be accepted, he honed his talents and skills. He quickly became a textbook overachiever.

National Honor Society, Division I school, Fortune 500 company, and vaulting up the ladder of success three rungs at a time became his mark. Allen is still proving to his father that he not only has the raw talent to be successful but that he *is* successful. Not that his father cares about it either way. The elder Mr. Evans died when Allen was still in high school. But not a day in Allen's life goes by without him sensing his father's ghost frowning over his shoulder.

His wife, Minya, is the daughter of immigrants. She was born after her parents had already established themselves in America. They were blessed by the land of opportunity but never forgot what it was like to live where there was little hope. They pushed their daughter to be the best. They thought their motives were pure. They meant it for good, but they inadvertently robbed Minya of rest. They did it by not teaching her how to accept defeat. She married a male clone of herself, and they've been winning ever since.

Well, almost.

Allen and Minya don't flaunt their wealth, but it's obvious that they have it. And they know their marriage would be in peril if they lost it. The reason they know this is because they nearly lost the majority of their fortune—and their relationship—about six years ago. Allen made what most stockbrokers would consider a shrewd purchase of three different and promising new e-business stocks. Unfortunately, these three were all promise but no punch. He had transferred the money to his broker without consulting Minya. When things went bad and there was no other choice, he informed his wife. That's when World War III broke out in their home.

To be fair to Minya, it was a substantial loss. But for both of them, it was an unbearable lesson in reality. Unfortunately they didn't do very well on this pop quiz. For a long period of time, Minya's confidence in Allen was shattered. Even more surprising was the depression that overwhelmed Allen. He couldn't believe he had come so close to losing it all.

Allen and Minya's son has a mildly deformed foot that has prevented him from making it on to a competitive traveling soccer team. After three games of watching his son limp around after the ball on a city league, Allen had had enough. He pulled his son off the team. The coach begged him to reconsider, but the pleas fell on deaf ears.

The Evanses aren't able to rest because they don't know how to lose. They are happy only when they are succeeding. Because success is always temporary, they push themselves and their son from one victory to the next. The laurel leaves wither on their restless heads. They are a family with much pride but little joy. Their home suffers because they have failed to appropriate the keys to genuine rest.

A Visit to Your Home

We leave behind seven restless families. Their houses might be on the best streets in their communities, but each family is stuck at a spiritual and emotional dead end. With the tour over, I wonder what we would see if we looked in on your family. Maybe traces of the problems frustrating our seven not-so-imaginary friends.

Let's get personal. Did you see yourself in any of these families? I suppose it'd be hard not to. Traits of families like yours and mine contribute to the collage we've called Hurried Street. Let's look at the seven telltale marks of a hurried home and then take time for some honest self-evaluation.

My home may be hurried if:
- ◆ We're so busy that we can't relax.
- ◆ We're uncomfortable with quiet.
- ◆ We're seldom satisfied with what we have.
- ◆ We live according to shifting moral standards.
- ◆ We're overworked and underappreciated.
- ◆ We worry about things we can't control.
- ◆ We aren't happy unless we're successful.

Like you, I'm concerned about the maddening pace our culture sets. I want to give my family the gift of rest—to be able to move off Hurried Street forever. Unless I've missed my guess, you'd probably like to do the same. How do we turn the tables in our favor? It starts with some tough but honest self-evaluation.

To get started, let's take an unhurried look at four common threads that run even deeper through hurried households.

The First Thread: An Inability to Believe

Our culture questions the power of God at the same time it emphasizes the adequacy of people. We are encouraged to reject the God who is there in order to become the gods we are not. Those of us committed to a personal God, a God actively involved in our lives, find ourselves in conflict with an environment that makes it too easy to doubt His power, grace, and sufficiency.

The Second Thread: A General Discontent

Being hurried and restless throws a wet blanket over our joy. It reminds me of a mild fever: you're not sick enough to stop what you're doing and go to bed, but it's impossible to enjoy much of what you *are* doing. The constant pushing and shoving of contemporary life does that to us. Eventually the confusion leads us to wrong conclusions about what real joy in life is. Like a nagging pebble in our shoe, restlessness makes it difficult to enjoy the scenery as we make our eighty-year hike through time.

The Third Thread: A Lack of Genuine Intimacy

Intimacy serves as the tempered strength that runs through each link of the family chain. With it a family can endure anything; without it just about anything can knock us down. Intimacy provides the immune system for the soul—it battles the psychological infections of discouragement, rejection, inadequacy, insignificance, and insecurity. Being assured of acceptance by the people closest to us gives us confidence. Confidence gives us the ability to endure. But rushed schedules rob us of the time needed to develop intimate relationships. Too many people are duped into thinking that a little bit of "quality" time compensates for the lack of "quantity." If time is anything, it is the oxygen of close relationships. Hurried lives suffocate intimacy. Fortunately, as we learn in the Scriptures what it means to be at rest, we'll discover several keys to developing the communication and intimacy that are missing in hurried homes.

The Fourth Thread: A Tendency to Control

When schedules are crowded, sleep is shortchanged, work is unreasonable, and the kids' demands are relentless, some of us try to solve our personal dilemmas by exercising high control over the people who surround us. We want them to relieve our tension, to help us carry our load (even if they're struggling to balance their own). A hurried life urges us to assume the right to run other people's lives, tell them how they ought to think and feel. We convince ourselves that it's in their best interests. But this kind of control brings out the worst in the people we love and complicates an already frustrating situation. If this pattern of usurping authority continues long enough in a marriage or in the relationships between parents and children, restlessness has its way.

Each of these common threads of unrest places family relationships in a straitjacket. Why then is it so easy to fall victim to the trap of a hurried home? What sets us off on a high-speed chase without a road map?

The Lure of a Hurried Home

It's funny how easily we can find ourselves in a fast-forward mind-set. It doesn't require conscious effort. Actually it's the logical outcome of the forces brought to bear on us each day. I see it in my own family. The Kimmels have found that being hurried comes naturally, while being at rest requires an ongoing appraisal of priorities. All of us who are serious about our spiritual lives and our family lives must purposefully counter the forces threatening our ability to maintain rest.

What are these forces? They're the same ones frustrating the parents and kids who come to my office for help. They're the ones that may be taking their toll on your family too.

A Hurried Home: Our Culture Values It

The first pressure comes from a society that values being hurried. We have grown accustomed to having everything *now*. We are the instant generation. We like to tell an intercom on the backside of a restaurant what we'd like for dinner and then expect someone to be holding it out the window by the time we pull our car forward. We take projects down to the wire because we know we can ship a package anywhere in the continental United States (and now abroad) within twenty-four hours. ATMs give us immediate cash. Microwave ovens give us instant meals. Online shopping gives us sudden debt.

We have a love affair with haste. We call it convenience, and there is no doubt that many of our modern conveniences have made some of the mundane duties of life more tolerable. But there is a subtle programming that goes on at the same time. It's not long before we start driving our lives the way we drive our cars—too fast.

The days of needing to stop by a movie rental store are over. Now you can call or order a movie online and have it delivered to your house. If we could just get the people who offer this convenience to open up a pizza delivery/dry cleaner in conjunction with this DVD service, we could save ourselves the hassle of having to answer the front door more than once! Forget that—just order through your cable box and TiVo it for later.

There's nothing wrong with convenience. Many conveniences have made our lives much better. It's just that sometimes we unwittingly allow these same conveniences to free us up to complicate our lives in a dozen new ways. And every year, our consumer-oriented culture invents hundreds of better services and devices that merely make it inconvenient or difficult to relax.

A Hurried Home: Business Rewards It

If our culture values being hurried, it's because *business rewards it*. The second pressure demanding a hurried lifestyle is not one we can easily alter. The business community too often holds the family hostage. Winning in the business arena requires that we stay ahead of the competition. Marriage and family commitments must accommodate the whims of the company president obsessed with outperforming his or her competition. Many workers would like very much to rearrange their priorities but don't dare say anything—they know they are too expendable to complain.

A major financial magazine a while back published interviews with the one hundred "most successful executives" in the country. Listen to a comment from a man who made the top ten:

> Reaching the level of business success that I have requires
> total commitment. If your family is too demanding, *get a
> new family*. That's what I did.

While I applaud this man's honesty, he deserves anything but praise for the way he left his family in the dust. He's not alone. It seems that each rung of the corporate ladder has its own set of new demands. Frequently a raise in salary represents a raise in anxiety—more money for more things and less time to enjoy them. If society is a German shepherd, business is often a pit bull.

A Hurried Home: The Media Exploits It

Business and society can't compete with the third pressure that deprives the contemporary family of rest: pressure from the media. Relentless in its pursuit of the American family, the media is the cultural architect of the hurried lifestyle. Its very existence depends on keeping us restless and discontent.

Reality shows take us to exotic places and show us great-looking people changing partners as casually as they change clothes. Prime-time dramas teach us that the essence of life is being rich, beautiful, and unsatisfied. Housewives often come across as desperate, and so many of the men seem lost. Savvy corporations create a toy or a doll or a video game and then build a cartoon around it—making our children feel inadequate if they don't have one of their very own. The proliferating cable news programs show us horrific pictures and tell us which politician is to blame, but they make it a professional practice to never offer singular solutions—just off-setting opinions. And if the shows themselves haven't convinced us, hundreds of all-too-eager advertisers make the good life too attractive to pass up—even if a family has to incur terminal debt to achieve it. And to make sure we don't leave home without temptation, we can download the whole hurried philosophy to our cell phones and iPods.

Speaking of television, for more than half a century, television has presented family problems in an unrealistic light. No matter how complicated the problem, we know that it will be solved in less than an hour with plenty of breaks to sell us a piece of the good life. Along the way we're programmed to think that problem solving is easier than it really is.

The Hurried Home: Sometimes the Church Encourages It

At some churches, the only qualification needed of a person placed in charge of the children's Sunday school department is a detectable pulse.

It's a shame that the one organism outside of our immediate home meant to provide a place of calm and rest can sometimes be one of its biggest challengers. There's tons of work and few willing souls to do it. That's been the nightmare of the church since it was established in the book of Acts. The handful of the faithful and the company of the committed are the ones who get called on over and over. I don't necessarily blame pastors. They're overworked too. Pastors oversee the work of ministry and ensure that it gets completed, and they must lean on gifted people to fill the gaps. But it's easy for a church to become too programmed and overscheduled, putting more religious food and ecclesiastical responsibility on a member's plate than he or she can really handle.

I was just about born in the church. Actually I was born on a Saturday night. Eight days later, I was in the church nursery. That's okay. Our family enjoyed church, and my parents were glad to serve. But it was easy to substitute our time together in church for our time together as a family. For the Kimmels, it was Sunday morning, Sunday night, and Wednesday night—no matter what.

Not long ago someone asked me about my best childhood memory. I was a little surprised at the first thought that jumped into my mind. It was of a cold Sunday in Pennsylvania. The snow had started to fall during Sunday school and had already accumulated about six inches by the time the sermon was over. Word around the narthex was that if it kept up they might have to cancel evening church.

I was stunned at the time. *Cancel evening church? Do you still get to go to heaven if you do that?* But sure enough, it was canceled. Late that afternoon, my father bundled up and walked down to a community store to get some supplies. (It was closed, but he'd called ahead to the people who lived above the store, and they let him in.) He brought home some Coca-Colas (a luxury for kids back then), potato chips, and a lot of other great stuff to wire four excited kids. Mom got out a big jigsaw puzzle, and Dad turned on *The Wonderful World of Disney*. After that we watched a popular western called *Maverick*. That was the only night in my entire childhood that I saw those two shows. Dad said that since school was going to be canceled, we could stay up until we dropped (with all that sugar and caffeine running through our veins, it would have been impossible to get us to sleep anyway). We put together puzzles, listened to records, sang, and told jokes until the wee hours.

It was the best evening I can remember from my childhood—and it wouldn't have happened if they hadn't canceled church.

Throughout this book you will read about my devotion to the church and the priority I place on it as an extension of our families. For me, church is a non-negotiable part of a rested heart. Most churches are sensitive to the needs of the family, and most pastors work to wisely steward the handful of compatible hours the average family has to devote to church activities. My words here are a reminder to us all that we can get so busy "doing church" that we lose its intended effect on our lives. If we aren't careful about this, the church we turn to for direction and perspective can easily become part of the problem it's supposed to be solving.

The Hurried Home: Our Egos Demand It

The truth is that I don't need society, a job, the media, or even the church to create a hurried home. I can do a great job of it on my own. The selfish human ego hungers for an overloaded life. We become addicted to regular surges of adrenaline.

Our hurried lifestyle is a result of taking shortcuts in life. Since the Fall of man in the Garden of Eden, sin has refused to let us rest. Stripped to its core, sin is the desire to have it now. It takes time to communicate meaningfully. It takes time to develop intimate friendships. It takes time to build character in a child. But sin is the enemy of time.

Warped by a misguided sense of need, our egos look for cheap short-cuts. And we end up restless and dissatisfied with life.

Yet God offers hope. The exciting truth for the modern family is that genuine rest can be enjoyed today. It's God's gift to the contemporary home, which is in desperate need of a break from the rat race.

For those of you who are feeling dismayed, take heart. I was dismayed until I realized that God has provided a strategy for countering the pressures of life in the HOV lane. In the next chapter, we'll lay the irreplaceable foundation for that strategy.

3

THE FOUNDATION
FOR GENUINE REST

Calamity has a sick sense of timing.

It doesn't believe in warnings, just surprises. It's not a stranger knocking at our front door, but a burglar coming in through a back window. Though I've been spared many visits by calamity, the few I've had have grabbed me by my spirit and shaken their instruction into the deepest recesses of my heart. What I learned one cold December night in a sterile hospital room you may learn in a different setting. But the lessons have universal application for any soul yearning for genuine rest.

While my wife, Darcy, was in the hospital recovering from the cesarean delivery of our third child, our other two children were left to my care. They didn't mask their anxiety as they watched their father trying to be mother. Frankly, their concerns had merit.

I've never really struggled with being a provider for my family. But when I have to not only bring home the bacon but cook it too, there is genuine cause for concern. My children know the extent of my skills in the kitchen. I can prepare a bowl of cereal, and I make a great batch of ice. I know the number for Domino's Pizza and the quickest route to

Chic-fil-A. Beyond that I come up lame at mealtime. Darcy was going to be in the hospital for five days. In my mind that calculated out to at least fifteen variations of cereal and ice—or a lot of fast food.

By the third night of my stint as Mr. Mom, I thought things were going pretty well. My kids had brushed a little harder to remove their french-fried breath, and we had shared bedtime prayers and a few choruses of "Jesus Loves Me" before both charges drifted off to dreamland. I crawled into my own bed and did a quick inventory of the day. As far as I was concerned, the day couldn't have gone better. I'd had a great time with my two oldest children, enjoyed an excellent visit with my wife and new daughter, gotten some work done at the office, cleaned the house, and even paid a few bills. It was satisfying to sink into a deep sleep knowing that everything was under control.

Now, my style of sleeping resembles a mild coma. I make such a commitment to the process of slumber that it takes a lot to shake me awake.

Somewhere a phone was ringing.

I incorporated it into my dreams for a suspended moment until its persistence drew me up from the depths. My clock radio said it was only 11:30 p.m., but I felt as if I'd been asleep for hours.

I groped for the phone. It was Darcy. She was crying.

Having been married to Darcy for a decade and a half, I'd become fairly good at recognizing whether her tears were of joy, hurt, or fear. Her unrestrained sobbing over the phone told me something was seriously wrong. She was terrified.

She had just been informed that our three-day-old daughter had stopped breathing…three times. The alert nurses had gotten her lungs going each time, but to be on the safe side they had her on a monitor.

In the time it took Darcy to transfer this information, my illusion of having everything under control was obliterated. When you hear that your child may have a physical malfunction, you immediately assume the worst. Maybe it's a subconscious defense mechanism: if we imagine the darkest scenario, we aren't surprised when it happens—and are over-joyed when it doesn't.

At that moment, however, Darcy needed my assurance that every-thing would be all right. The calming and confident words I spoke into the phone contradicted the worry that was knotting my insides. We prayed together, giving the whole situation to God. My voice was even and steady. I was a tower of spiritual strength—until I hung up. Then I reverted to being human. My courage turned to Jell-O. I was a man with words for others but none for myself. My heart literally ached inside my chest.

When a loved one is hurting or in danger, our first desire is to *do* something. To find yourself helpless in such a moment is one of the worst feelings imaginable. I was prepared to scale a wall, run a marathon, fight an army. But just sit there and *wait*?

I knew the pain wasn't going to subside if I remained at home and did nothing. Besides, I suddenly wasn't very tired. I called my brother, who came over to stay with my sleeping kids, and then I jumped into my car and sped off through the darkness to Scottsdale Memorial Hospital.

Hospitals take on their own personality at night. When I walked into the maternity wing, the normal rush that accompanies labor and delivery had given way to a quiet calm. Nurses spoke in low, deliberate tones. Music hummed faintly from a radio at the nurses' station. Every-one seemed to tiptoe. As I walked down the line of half-opened doors, I could see exhausted mothers trying to get one more decent night of sleep before they returned home to face several months of night shifts. I checked in with Darcy to let her know that I was there and that the kids were covered at home and then headed down the hall to the NICU. The door whispered open.

Tiny Plexiglas beds held tightly wrapped little bodies—each rep-resenting the hopes and goals of moms and dads scattered across Phoenix. All of those little sleepers were important, but one bundle drew me to its side like a magnet. A small face with tightly shut eyes protruded from the end of a soft, pink flannel cocoon. The wires snaking out from underneath the covers ran to a cluster of machines monitoring her vital signs.

The doctor briefed me, speculating on what might be causing our daughter's struggle to maintain normal breathing. Then he left and I sat down to watch, wait, and think.

Apnea. Well, there was a new word for my vocabulary. The dictionary defines it as "a transient cessation of respiration." But I didn't have the benefit of a dictionary definition that night. My introduction to the word came from the piercing alarm of a heart and lung monitor. Apnea defined itself a dozen times during the night and each time brought the issue of life and death into glaring focus. Most of us take the involuntary cadence of our heart and lungs for granted—until it becomes tentative. Watching the inconsistent dancing lines on the monitor made me realize what a tiny thread normal life hangs on.

I maintained my fatherly vigil for the next seven hours, alternating between watching the baby, and praying, and rocking the baby, and praying. Predicaments like these are natural times for contemplation. It's amazing how much perspective you can gain on your crisis if given the luxury of being undisturbed for a few hours. I rocked back and forth in the silence, feeling the warmth of my baby girl's life through the blanket.

The night nurse attending the handful of infants in the nursery made me comfortable. She brought me a cup of coffee, and we exchanged brief small talk. She commented that she had seen many fathers spend nights sitting next to their children. I told her that I realized my being there was not so much for my daughter's benefit as for mine. She understood. Love was driving me to search for hope.

I might be a trained seminarian and communicator, but somehow the comforting wisdom of practical theology seemed far from my thoughts. I was a father feeling the myriad of mixed emotions that play in your heart when you watch your own flesh and blood struggling to win the first fight of her life.

Inner Needs

The crisis I experienced at my little daughter's side forced me to consider this matter of *rest* as I had never considered it before. Somehow I knew that if I was ever going to entertain the notion of genuine rest in my life—or in my daughter's—its certainty would depend on my ability to find rest in that very situation. On that very battlefield. On that very night.

It was a battle on two fronts: a restlessness on the outside created by circumstances beyond my control and a restlessness on the inside created by my struggle with doubt and fear. I wanted to win on both fronts, but I knew that victory over the battle inside me was the best way to ensure victory over the battle against my circumstances.

As I wondered if my daughter would live to experience even a portion of the hopes and dreams my wife and I had for her, I was taken back to the grass-roots issues of life. It wasn't important to me that she become a great pianist or master several languages; it was becoming clear that life boiled down to a handful of basic needs.

In fact, at the foundation of the concept of human rest are three inner needs. We build our lives on and around them. They are powerful needs that demand satisfaction and are as essential to our survival as food, clothing, and shelter. If they are met in legitimate, healthy ways, we can experience sweet contentment. Deny ourselves any or all of these needs and we put in place all the ingredients necessary for a restless life.

I settled into the rocking chair and stared at the little life in my arms. She was so new. Yet given a chance, her life would become a complicated blend of emotions, impressions, and experiences. But just as the various hues of the rainbow are merely blended shades of three primary colors, the complexities that make up life are only variations of three inner needs. Love, purpose, and hope were what my little girl needed in order to feel complete.

Those three needs that I wanted so much to satisfy in her life as she grew older were the same needs I needed fulfilled in myself if I ever wished to enjoy genuine rest.

Security: The Need for Love

There is probably no greater inner pain than the pain of loneliness. Our culture has popularized the cult of self-worship, but it is an empty shrine. We can make macho speeches or play self-sufficient games, but our independent attitude is a thin veneer at best. Deep within every living soul is a gnawing need to be accepted.

We are made so by design. God put a perfect man in a perfect environment…yet Adam was lonely. Fashioned to be incomplete by himself, his heart longed for companionship. And it was because of his longing that God made a woman for him to love. Eve completed a heart that was meant to be bonded with another.

It's probably no colossal revelation that people need love. The carved initials in trees lining elementary school playgrounds testify that the need for loving commitment begins early. It's not enough to have friends; we need *best* friends. And the pain experienced when the covenant of friendship is broken is the worst pain of all.

"Love is a two-way street," croons the country singer, "but my baby's changing lanes." A healthy person never gets good at being jilted. The thousandth time you're rejected hurts just as deeply as the first. So fundamental is humankind's need for love that when it is denied, it can cause a person to struggle emotionally, physically, intellectually, and spiritually—especially if it is withheld or denied in the early formative years of a child's life.

As a father drawn to a child in need, I was keenly aware of my own inner need for love. I knew that my ability to experience rest had contingencies. I had to know that I was loved—and I had to feel freedom in loving back. Minor or serious, my daughter's physical problems would seem insignificant to her if she had to go through life feeling unloved. The inner need for love was one area of her life in which I couldn't afford to fail.

Significance: The Need for Purpose

Love is a driving need that, when met, gives a person a deep sense of security, but we need purpose to feel significant. We need that little spark of attention from someone who believes in us. The mileage that the human spirit can derive from an affirming word is endless.

Most great achievers fall into two categories: they either have a purpose and are motivated to live it out, or they are madly driven to find one. Innate within the concept of rest is a confidence that you are significant. A gifted classical musician comes to mind.

At the age of seventy-two, Andor Foldes recalled how praise made all the difference for him early in his career. His first recollection of an affirming word was at age seven, when his father kissed him and thanked him for helping in the garden. And he remembered it more than *six decades later* as though it were yesterday.

But the account of another kiss that changed his life says a great deal about our inner drive for significance. At age sixteen, living in Budapest, Foldes was already a skilled pianist. But he was experiencing a personal low because of a conflict with his piano teacher. In the midst of that very troubled year, however, one of the most renowned pianists of the day came to the city to perform. Emil von Sauer was famous not only because of his abilities at the piano but because he could claim the notoriety of being the last surviving pupil of Franz Liszt.

Sauer requested that young Foldes play for him. Foldes obliged the master with some of the most difficult works of Bach, Beethoven, and Schumann. When Foldes had finished, Sauer walked over to him and kissed him on the forehead.

"My son," he said, "when I was your age, I became a student of Liszt.

He kissed me on the forehead after my first lesson, saying, 'Take good care of this kiss—it comes from Beethoven, who gave it to me after hearing me play.' I have waited for years to pass on this sacred heritage, but now I feel you deserve it."[2]

Foldes no longer had a personal crisis. His kiss from Beethoven gave him a new sense of purpose.

When the internal well of confidence is dry, we all need a kiss of affirmation. The problem that caused my brand-new daughter's fight to breathe had drained my confidence. I wanted to rest in the reality of my significance and hers, but it was difficult to see past my doubts.

Strength: The Need for Hope

The trilogy of our inner needs is not complete without hope. Hope is the environment in which love and purpose breed contentment. It is the third strand, and it gives grit and strength to our security and significance.

What good is it to make great time on a road to nowhere? Too many people are confused into thinking that a kind word and a sense of direction are enough. But hope is the glimmer of light on the horizon that says there is a reason to keep moving forward. The light might be faint and the road long, but the trip is bearable if we're certain there is a destination.

Hopes and *dreams* are often used as synonyms. In the Cinderella world so many people occupy, living happily ever after is followed by rudely waking up to reality. Hope has to be more than that.

If dreams are made of sand, then hope is made of concrete. It's the bulkhead that withstands the pounding waves of life's stormy seas. It's the belief in the back of our minds that assures our spirits. But it must have a divine touch to last. Hope that is a product of human intuition is temporal, but those who allow God's love to cast its cross-shaped shadow over their human spirit give hope eternal life.

Love, purpose, and hope paid me a hospital visit that night. They weren't abstract concepts floating around in my brain. They were three friends wanting to settle down in my heart.

A Lesson from the Past

God has peculiar ways of bringing insight to our minds. With my daughter lying beside me and my thoughts focused on what life really means, two songs from two very different men came to mind. One played in my ears, and the other played in my heart. The songs conveyed the same message, but because of the men singing them, they stood in conspicuous contrast.

One man's story ended at a grave; the other's began there.

Up to that point, I hadn't been paying attention to the music coming from the radio at the nurses' station. Most of the songs blended in with the background noises of the nursery. But my ears perked up when I heard the sleepy deejay introduce the next song he was about to play.

"Here's one for all of you who would like to be asleep, but your troubles are keeping you awake."

He probably had to do some searching in the station archives to find it, but once the song started to play, I had to agree that its message was for me. The musical relic was vintage Elvis Presley, but it had some advice for a confused father sitting beside his infant daughter in a quiet Arizona hospital.

Elvis was singing his hit "Crying in the Chapel." I hadn't heard the song in quite some time, and I found myself drawn to its message in a new way. The final lines had the most encouragement for me:

Take your troubles to the chapel.
Get down on your knees and pray.[3]

Inner peace is a gift God wants to give us in the middle of our crises. "Crying in the Chapel" was a reminder to me that God is a sanctuary for restless, troubled hearts.

But the song's message was lost on the singer.

I've always had a hard time disassociating a message from its messenger. I couldn't help wondering how it was that Elvis could be so effective at delivering advice and such a failure at taking it.

The Tomb of the "King"

When America was informed that "the king of rock and roll" was dead, millions of fans went into mourning. For more than two decades, Elvis Presley had embodied the soul of a young generation that wanted to shake, rattle, and roll. He lived too fast and died too soon.

When you look back over the life of a media phenomenon the size of Elvis, it's hard to separate truth from fiction. Some fans were and still are so blindingly loyal that they don't want their memories muddied by facts. But the circumstances surrounding Elvis's death give us a picture of the anguish that plagued him most of his life.

He went from rags to riches on the wings of music. His controversial records and performances brought scorn from parents, accolades from teenagers, and money from both. Once his music became a mainstay, Elvis rode the popularity tidal wave with amazing skill.

He was generous. Never forgetting his humble beginnings, Elvis was quick to cheer on the underdogs and reward those who touched his life. When someone did him a favor, he paid that person back a thousandfold.

He was religious. His musical eyeteeth were cut on the church hymnal. He knew that a dimension of his life needed and wanted God. Because we're people who want to believe the best about our heroes, the public's view of Elvis's spiritual life is probably exaggerated. But we know that he acknowledged his need and desire for God at various times in his life.

He was personable. Those who knew him well saw him as an intensely fragile man. His circle of friends was small, and his demands on them were great. With the responsibility of being his friend came the privilege of being loved back. The handful of people who got close to him testified to the seriousness he placed on being a friend. He was loyal and sensitive.

But all was not well inside the heart of "the king." Having everything money could buy wasn't enough. Though surrounded by fans everywhere he went, he spent the prime years of his life overwhelmed by loneliness, even with the handful of friends who stood close by him. His life is a striking illustration that wealth and fame do not complete us. Elvis needed to love and be loved; he needed a sense of purpose and an assurance of hope.

He is proof that inner peace isn't for sale. As his popularity grew and his bank accounts' bottom line stretched from seven digits to eight, Elvis's restlessness intensified. He could not find calm for his anxious spirit. His life echoed the words of his own song: he searched and he searched, but he couldn't find…

Elvis saw his enemy every time he looked in a mirror. He didn't need unforeseen calamities to bring him down. He did an adequate job of destroying himself without the help of outside circumstances. He had choices to make but no adequate guide to use when making them. In the end, his choices cost him everything. The only distinction between Elvis and most other people overwhelmed by anxiety was that he was forced to live out his frustration with millions of people watching.

Elvis Presley died long before he needed to. Ravaged by drugs, the heart inside this media-made king gave out. When his unconscious body was found lying on the floor at Graceland, it marked the end of years of restlessness. He had all of what the world said should give us rest. But in the end, none of it could save him.

I rocked back and forth in my chair in the nursery. Elvis's song made me sad for him. I remembered watching the news the day they buried him at Graceland. The line of mourners snaked out past his Memphis home for several city blocks. They were stunned that their king would leave them so soon. Years later, they still come, filing silently past his grave.

And then, as Elvis's song faded from the radio, I thought of another grave. A tiny plot in a simple cemetery on the edge of the Arizona desert. There are no street signs directing you to the grave site or crowds of mourners to mark its presence. The few times I've visited, I've had a hard time finding it. But to the west of the pond and just a few feet from a lonely tree, the blades of Bermuda grass are briefly interrupted to allow a modest, gentle statement carved in granite to peek through:

PUNKIN'
In loving memory
Jennifer Marie Strader
August 11, 1975–December 13, 1984

It's one of the few physical reminders that this little girl existed. But her brief life made an unforgettable impression on her family and friends, and her parents' courage after her death gave me one of the best reasons why I'm sure we can have rest no matter what.

"There Is Peace"

Resting my head against the back of the rocker, I closed my eyes and found myself humming a different song. The words and music were written by a special friend—Jennifer's father, Rodger Strader. When he wrote the song, he was a happily married young man with three children. He couldn't know that two years later he would have only two children to come home to at night. You see, Rodger Strader's song was prophetic, and in his loneliest moment, its message gave him rest.

Sacred musicians may not have the fame and fortune of their counterparts in the secular music industry, but they have the same needs. When Rodger began his career as a Christian songwriter and singer, he wanted to love and be loved; he wanted to sense a purpose in his life and be stirred by the hope that he wrote and sang about. Next to his confidence in Christ, his family made the biggest contribution to meeting those needs. His wife, Candy, came from a hymn-writer's family and understood the price creative talents must pay to draw powerful messages from their souls and put them to music. Rodger wrote beautiful songs, and Candy raised beautiful children. Their daughter, Jennifer, was sandwiched between two handsome sons.

Singing about hope is a whole lot easier than believing in it, especially when one of your main reasons for living is suddenly and tragically removed from your life. Rodger's concept of hope was tested to its limits during the Christmas season of his daughter's ninth year.

It had seemed like such a routine day. Candy and her sister pulled up in front of the school that afternoon, just as they did every weekday. The five kids they were collecting at school came from the four corners of the campus. The last to get into the car was Jennifer.

Jennifer wasn't an extrovert, but she wasn't an introvert either. She had one of those mild dispositions that blended easily with everyone. Because she had the heart and soul of a peacemaker, friendships were made and maintained with ease. She was a pretty and quiet little girl content with learning all the mysteries of childhood.

At a familiar corner, during a textbook left turn, tragedy paid a visit to the Strader family. A young man ran a red light and buried his truck into the side of the Straders' car. Jennifer's aorta was severed on impact, and her spirit immediately raced into the arms of the God she loved. Injuries to the others were repaired with time, but for Rodger and Candy, a hole was left in their hearts that time could not affect.

The Christmas season is a busy time for Christian musicians, especially if you've written popular Christmas musicals. Rodger was in Salem, Oregon, rehearsing one of his musicals with a metropolitan church choir when he received the phone call that all parents dread.

Rodger instantly became an expert on the power of words. "There's been an accident, and Jennifer didn't make it." Nine common words taken from everyday language were put in an order he had never heard or wanted to hear. When his brain interpreted them, Rodger's heart instantly broke. Words crushed his confident spirit with the force of a hammer. Rodger was surrounded by a stunned choir who shared a love for his Lord. But in spite of their circle of support, Rodger felt completely alone.

Had he arrived at the airport a few minutes earlier, he would've caught the last plane to Phoenix. Instead, his uncertainty was compounded by the pain of waiting. His wife and boys had been injured, and he wouldn't feel confident about the extent of their injuries until he could appraise them for himself. But one truth was a dark certainty: his little girl was lying in a Phoenix funeral home, and nothing was going to change that fact.

A friend back in Phoenix sent a private jet to fetch him from Portland. He sat in the back of the plane with only the noise of the engines and the endless night to keep him company. His mind jumped from worry about his wife and sons to memories of his Jennifer.

Stillness gives a spirit the ability to condense and compress a lifetime into a moment. The nine years of Jennifer Marie Strader's life danced across the screen in his mind. She had joined Rodger's walk through time when he was twenty-three and left when he was thirty-two, but the time that she had shared the path with him had made him a different man. A better man.

A little girl doesn't take up much space physically, but her personality can stretch to every corner of a house. When Rodger retrieved his wife and sons from his father-in-law's house and brought them home, it seemed that everywhere he looked he saw Jennifer. The artwork in her room and the projects she had left unfinished gave him an ache in his heart that made him want to groan out loud. He found himself wishing she would come walking into his study to ask for help with her homework.

Quiet can be an enemy to the broken heart, but it can also become an ally. The silence that stepped in where Jennifer had stepped out was the silence in which Rodger Strader ultimately found rest. In the stillness of his study, Rodger turned to the Inspiration of his songs, the Author of his soul. He had prayed a hundred times in the twenty-four hours since his daughter's death, but the whirlwind of events surrounding the tragedy hadn't allowed him the luxury of inner rest. With the boys tucked into their beds and his wife finally slipping off to sleep in hers, Rodger retired to his study.

Rest is a visitor from heaven that wants to meet us in our tragedies. Unfortunately there's something about our human pride that crowds this visitor out. Rodger had been gifted with great emotional strength, and normally he could handle his problems. But this was too big for his defenses. Rodger found release. He wept. He poured out his pain before God. God gave him rest—using familiar words and a familiar musical theme. Rodger crossed the room to his stereo and cued up a well-known song.

The singer began the lines Rodger had written two years before. He heard the song this time as if it were brand-new. It was as though the song hadn't been written *by* him as much as *for* him. The verses he had written by watching other people's pain had new meaning. He hung on to them as if hearing them for the first time:

In a world that's wracked by sin and sorrow,
    there is peace.
When you find no hope for your tomorrow,
    there is peace.[4]

Rodger was overwhelmed by a calm that came from above. Humbly, he accepted God's gift of rest for his tired soul. It was like a soothing salve from the hand of God: *My grace is sufficient for you, Rodger, because My power is perfected in your weakness.*

A few days later, Rodger and Candy took their last look at the body that was once home to their daughter. They faced their darkest hour with a courage and dignity only God could supply. They learned the foundational principle of rest that would carry them through the lonely years of adjustment that followed Jennifer's death. That principle is the realization that *rest is a choice*.

In many of our trials there is no rest *from*, but there is rest *in*. Jesus said:

> Come to me, all you who are weary and burdened, and I will give you rest. Take my yoke upon you and learn from me, for I am gentle and humble in heart, and you will find rest for your souls. (Matthew 11:28–29)

The Lord's words are timeless. They stretch across twenty centuries to meet a couple standing by a child's simple grave and settle in the spirit of a confused father watching an infant fight to take her first fragile breaths. They reassure us that our quest for rest is reachable. But it has to start *within* us before it can move *outside* of us. The pressures that create restless spirits can be countered by divine non-negotiables for genuine rest. But these external solutions assume that we first have accepted God's internal solutions.

- ◆ He loves us.
- ◆ He made us with a purpose.
- ◆ He guarantees us hope.

Rest is an attitude based on truth we're certain of regardless of doubts. It's a deposit our mind makes to the accounts of our hearts when we know the pressures aren't going to be quickly removed. We claim rest more often and exercise it more regularly when we view it as a strategy for persevering rather than as an escape from reality.

We may learn the attitude of rest vicariously by watching cherished friends go through the nightmare of death, or we may learn it during an anxious night rocking a sick child. But its lessons *must* be learned.

God's rest doesn't imply that we won't ever grieve or feel anguish, but it does guarantee that we'll hurt differently. It's a divinely altered perspective that won't let us lose sight of the fact that we are loved, even at the depth of our despair.

The Dawn Always Comes

I was still rocking my daughter when the hospital started to wake up. A fresh batch of coffee and nurses signaled the beginning of a new day. I had endured my first all-night vigil with one of my children. Somehow I felt that I would have a few more of these before the last one left home, but I wasn't really fearful anymore. The alarms on the monitor had sounded several times that night, and with each one my heart rushed. Apnea signals had been counted, and intermittent heartbeats had been recorded on my daughter's chart. But as the dawn approached, I was calm.

My body hadn't left my child's side, but my heart had been to heaven. The two musicians who ministered to me had taught me a lot about what rest is and what it isn't. I was calm about my daughter's condition. It wasn't some foolish mind game that says, *If I believe she'll be all right, then she will.* Life is a vapor. There are no guarantees. My daughter's condition was treatable, and hopefully she would outgrow it. (She did.) But Jennifer Strader was proof enough that rest doesn't require a happy ending.

The rest that overwhelmed me came from a God who knows the pain of despair firsthand:

He who did not spare his own Son, but gave him up for us all—how will he not also, along with him, graciously give us all things? (Romans 8:32)

A bloodstained cross and an empty tomb are the only guarantees. And they make choosing rest easier.

I went by my wife's room to encourage her and then headed for home. On the way out I slipped into the nursery once more to plant a kiss on my little girl. The name scrawled on the card taped to her bed was a new one to me. My wife and I had decided on it a few days before she was born. Since her birth, we'd had second thoughts about the name. But after the lessons she had taught me that night, I couldn't think of calling her anything else. Her name is from the Old Testament. It means "rest" and "tranquillity."

I bent down and kissed her on her tiny head.

"Thanks for the seminar on rest, *Shiloh*," I whispered. "Now wake up and start practicing your breathing."

PART

2

A FORGIVING SPIRIT

The First Necessity

For reasons I've never quite figured out, I was thirty-four years old before I saw my first animated Disney movie. My oldest daughter had accompanied me on a week-long speaking engagement, but bad weather was making it hard for us to enjoy the outdoors. While exploring the local town, we discovered that their only movie theater was showing Disney's *The Jungle Book* during the matinee. We went to see it on a Tuesday and ended up going back twice more.

One of the more memorable songs of the film was a toe-tapping tune by a fun-loving bear named Baloo. This clumsy fellow danced around the jungle singing, "The Bare Necessities," and it was hard to keep my daughter from getting up and dancing around the theater. For ol' Baloo, happiness consisted of a few necessities: a banana, some good music, and a strong tree to scratch his back against.

In our stressful and demanding culture, rest is also found in a handful of necessities. It's not restricted to the experts in time management or those fortunate enough to enjoy large chunks of discretionary time. It goes to those willing to continually maintain a few bare necessities.

As I study the Bible, I am continually impressed by six clear characteristics that separate the rested heart from the restless. These characteristics are non-negotiable principles—essential if you want to enjoy a calm and rested spirit on an ongoing basis. I distilled them down by studying Jesus under stress.

Curse of the Living Dead

A person who is unable or unwilling to forgive can never be truly at rest. In fact, the number-one cause of an anxious heart is unresolved disappointment in others.

As deeply as we may long for peace and rest, many of us find the corridors of our hearts haunted by ghosts from the past. Walking corpses. Grotesque, bitter spirits that moan and linger and rattle their chains—all because we have refused to forgive people who have done us wrong.

How important is this? Allow me to introduce you to several men and women in an obscure little church outside Seoul, South Korea, who can testify to the anguish that results when we refuse to forgive.

A careful student of that region's history will note that Koreans have not always been known for hostility toward their neighbors, especially in their history prior to World War II. For the most part, they have been a peace-loving people. Yet they have found themselves consistently under attack by surrounding nations throughout their existence.

Shortly after the end of the Russo-Japanese War in 1905, Japan invaded and occupied Korea. Of all Korea's oppressors, Japan was the most ruthless. For forty years they overwhelmed the Koreans with brutality that would sicken the strongest of stomachs. Their crimes against women and children were inhuman. Many Koreans still live with physical and emotional scars from the Japanese occupation.

One group singled out for concentrated oppression was the Christians. When the Japanese army overpowered Korea, one of the first things they did was board up the evangelical churches and eject most foreign missionaries. It has always fascinated me how people fail to learn from history. Conquering nations have consistently felt that shutting up churches would shut down Christianity. It didn't work in Rome when the church was established, and it hasn't worked since. Yet somehow the Japanese thought this time would be different.

The conquerors started by banning church meetings and jailing many of the key Christian spokesmen. The oppression intensified as the Japanese military increased its profile in the South Pacific. The Land of the Rising Sun spread its influence through a reign of savage brutality. Anguish filled the hearts of the oppressed and kindled hatred deep in their souls.

One pastor persistently entreated his local Japanese police chief for permission to meet for services. His nagging was finally accommodated, and the police chief offered to unlock his church—for one meeting.

It didn't take long for word to travel. Committed Christians starving for an opportunity for unhindered worship quickly made plans. Long before dawn on that promised Sunday, Korean families throughout the region made their way to the church. They passed by the watchful eyes of their Japanese captors, but nothing was going to steal their joy. As they closed the doors behind them, they shut out the cares of oppression and shut in passionate spirits restless to glorify their Lord.

The Korean church has always had a reputation as a singing church, and on this day their voices of praise could not be concealed inside the little wooden sanctuary. Song after song rang through the open windows into the bright Sunday morning. For a handful of peasants listening nearby, the final two songs seemed to become suspended in time.

It was during a stanza of "Nearer, My God, to Thee" that the Japanese police chief waiting outside gave the orders. The people toward the back of the church could hear them barricade the doors, but no one realized that they had doused the church with kerosene until they smelled the smoke. The dried wooden skin of the small church quickly ignited.

Fumes filled the structure as tongues of flame began to lick the baseboard on the interior walls.

There was an immediate rush for the windows. But momentary hope recoiled in horror as the men climbing out the windows came crashing back in—their bodies ripped by a hail of bullets.

The good pastor knew it was the end.

With a calm that comes from confident faith, he led his congregation in a hymn whose words served as a fitting farewell to earth and a loving salutation to heaven. The first few words were all the prompting the terrified worshipers needed. With smoke burning their eyes, they joined as one to sing their hope and leave their legacy.

Their song became a serenade to the horrified and helpless witnesses outside. Their words also tugged at the hearts of the cruel men who oversaw this flaming execution of the innocent:

Alas! and did my Savior bleed?
    And did my Sovereign die?
Would He devote that sacred head
    For such a worm as I?

Just before the roof collapsed, the helpless congregation sang the last verse, their words an eternal testimony to their faith:

But drops of grief can ne'er repay
    The debt of love I owe:
Here, Lord, I give myself away.
    'Tis all that I can do!

At the cross, at the cross where I first saw the light,
    And the burden of my heart rolled away—
It was there by faith I received my sight,
    And now I am happy all the day.[5]

The strains of music and the wails of children were lost in a roar of flames. Elements that had once formed bone and flesh mixed with the smoke and dissipated into the air. Bodies that once housed life fused with the charred rubble of a building that once housed a church. But the souls who left singing finished their chorus in the throne room of God.

Clearing the incinerated remains was the easy part. Erasing the hate would take decades. For the relatives of the victims, this carnage was too much. Evil had stooped to a new low, and there seemed to be no way to curb their bitter loathing of the Japanese.

In the decades that followed, that bitterness was passed on to a new generation. The Japanese, although conquered, remained a hated enemy. The monument the Koreans built at the location of the fire not only memorialized those who had died but stood as a mute reminder of their pain.

Inner rest?

How could rest coexist with bitterness as deep as marrow in the bones?

Suffering, of course, is part of life. People hurt people. Almost all of us have experienced it at some time. Maybe you felt it when you came home to find that your spouse had abandoned you, or when your integrity was destroyed by a series of well-timed lies, or when your company was bled dry by a partner. It kills you inside. Bitterness clamps down on your soul like iron shackles.

The Korean people who found it too hard to forgive could not enjoy the "peace that passes all understanding." Hatred choked their joy. It wasn't until 1971 that hope arrived.

A group of Japanese pastors traveling through Korea came upon the memorial. When they read the details of the tragedy and the names of the spiritual brothers and sisters who had perished, they were overcome with shame. Their country had sinned, and even though none of them had been personally involved (some hadn't even been born at the time of the tragedy), they still felt a national guilt that could not be excused.

The pastors returned to Japan committed to righting a wrong. There was an immediate outpouring of love from their fellow believers. They raised ten million yen (at the time about twenty-five thousand USD). The money was then transferred through the proper channels, and a beautiful white church building was erected on the site of the tragedy.

When the dedication service for the new building was held, a delegation from Japan joined the families as special guests. Although their generosity was acknowledged and their attempts at making peace appreciated, the memories were still there. Hatred preserves pain. It keeps the wounds open and the hurts fresh. The Koreans' bitterness had festered for decades. Christian brothers or not, these Japanese were descendants of a ruthless enemy.

The speeches were made, the details of the tragedy recalled, and the names of the dead honored. It was time to bring the service to a close. Someone in charge of the service thought it would be appropriate to conclude with the same two songs that were sung the day the original church was burned. The worship leader began singing the words of "Nearer, My God, to Thee."

Something remarkable happened as the voices mingled with the familiar melody. As the memories of the past mixed with the truth of the song, resistance started to melt. The inspiration that had given hope to a doomed collection of churchgoers in a past generation gave hope once more.

The song leader closed the service with the hymn "At the Cross."

The normally stoic Japanese could not contain themselves. The tears that had begun to fill their eyes during the song suddenly gushed from deep inside. They turned to their Korean spiritual relatives and begged them for forgiveness.

The guarded, callous hearts of the Koreans were not quick to surrender. But the love of the Japanese believers—unintimidated by decades of hatred—tore at the Koreans' emotions.

At the cross, at the cross, where I first saw the light,
    And the burden of my heart rolled away...

One Korean turned toward a Japanese brother. Then another. And then the floodgates holding back a wave of emotion let go. The Koreans met their new Japanese friends in the middle. They clung to each other and wept. Japanese tears of repentance and Korean tears of forgiveness intermingled to bathe the site and cleanse it of an old nightmare.

Heaven had sent the gift of reconciliation to a little church in Korea.

Dealing with the Memories

The degree that you and I are open to experiencing inner rest is easily determined. It is equally proportionate to our willingness to forgive and be forgiven. Some of you reading these words need not search any further to find out why you aren't experiencing inner rest.

Unresolved conflict, cutting words, cruel rumors, and an isolated heart because of rejection siphon the joy away from even the most beautiful moments of life. The rest you long for runs ahead of you like a rainbow forever out of reach. Maybe a few examples from people I've visited with will remind you of what I mean:

- ◆ You're taking a brief vacation from your shopping. You sit down in a Starbucks to enjoy some inner quiet when you hear a voice that spoils your solitude. The voice belongs to the boy who got your seventeen-year-old daughter pregnant. His next victim is hanging on his arm as he plops down at the other end of coffee shop. All you can remember is his reaction to the news that he was going to be a father: "Here's twenty bucks—why don't you get an abortion!" Your rage has bordered on homicidal ever since.

◆ Your husband didn't say good-bye. He didn't leave a note. He just squeezed the trigger, and it was over. You're not sure who you hate the most—him for leaving you that way or you for not being able to help him.

◆ He's a faithful grandfather. Never misses one of your son's soccer games. But you can't stand the sight of him there on the sidelines cheering your son because when you were wearing a childhood uniform and racing down the sidelines, you could never hear his voice shouting you on to victory. You have time for your child. Why didn't he have time for you?

◆ There they sit, as if nothing happened. Every Sunday they're frustratingly conspicuous in church. Her wardrobe is current and expensive. They jump into a fine car and go home to a fine house. But their lifestyle was financed by many people in the church who took out second mortgages or handed over their life savings. The "opportunity" turned out to be a scam, and the dream became a nightmare. Now he is safely guarded from repayment by convenient chapters of the bankruptcy code.

◆ She borrowed your car. You were glad to help. Of course, she didn't mean to wreck it; it was obviously an accident. But the insurance didn't cover all the repairs. And the person who wrecked the car felt that, because your financial resources were greater than hers, you could pay the deductible yourself. You see her every now and then driving around town. She waves from her brand-new car.

You get the point. We all have hurt that loves to come back and steal our joy. It sits in the back of our memories waiting for an opportunity to be recalled. It's always there, and no matter how hard we try, we can't remove it. There are countless advantages to being human rather than a computer, but sometimes it would be nice to have all of our painful memories stored on some external hard drive stuck in the side of our head. A few simple moves and you could either disconnect the hard drive or simply delete the hurt.

Even though we can't erase the hurts that lie stored on the permanent hard drive of our memories, we *can* offset their negative impact. In chemistry, if I want to neutralize an acid, I must counter with the equivalent of an opposite substance. Forgiveness works the same way. It's an alkaline nullifying the acidic nature of bitterness. It's that balancing presence that says, "You can remind me of my pain, but you can't rob me of my rest."

Bitterness is a slave master. It controls us. It demands too much.

And if we don't deal with our unresolved conflicts, they'll deal with us.

The requirements for maintaining anger and resentment are steep. You have to overtax friendships, ruin special events that could've become great memories, make your kids' lives miserable, get bad reviews at work for allowing your personal life to affect your job performance, prejudge new relationships, isolate yourself from people who need you, and neutralize the impact of God's Word in your life.

Bitterness affects us physically too. It might reward us with a miserable night's sleep or an upset stomach. It might spoil our appetite or drive us to eat too much. The relationship between physical health and inner joy is obvious. The unresolved anger and hurt festering in some people's hearts guarantee them a rough ride to the morgue. Those feelings also promise to get them there sooner.

It's easy to read what's on your mind at this moment. All I have to do is read my own. You're thinking of the pain you've endured—pain that seems too intense to forgive. I know how you feel. I think of some of the people who have had fun at my expense, who have attempted to move up the career ladder by trying to climb over me and then kick me off. I think of friends who said they'd be there and weren't. I've felt the cold steel of betrayal slipping into my back. And I've experienced the empty feeling that overwhelms you when you realize that the hand shoving it in is the hand of a friend.

I've had the same choices that face all people. I could be haunted and hounded by hurt, or I could forgive. If I make the choice to forgive, it's not because of some intrinsic good in me. I'm just as capable of revenge as the next guy. My decision to forgive is more motivated by need and desperation.

The Hill of Forgiveness

When the crimes against my heart seem unforgivable, I am compelled to take a walk up a hill. Hurting hearts all over the world have learned the power that is gained by taking this same walk. We may start in the savannas of East Africa, the frozen tundra of Siberia, or the congested sidewalks of Manhattan. Regardless of where we begin our trek, the paths merge at the base of the same hill. It's the Hill of Forgiveness that sits at the center of civilization. The ground at the top is level. The grass growing around the wooden stanchion and crossbeam ripples in the fresh breeze of freedom. There's always room for anyone wanting help for their hurt.

The cross is the single most significant symbol of forgiveness in history. Made by men and used by God, it is the hallmark of man at his worst and God at His best. God gifted man with keen intellect and abundant natural resources. He buried ore in the ground and stood timber in the forest. Man uncovered that ore. He melted and molded it into spikes. Man cut down that timber and shaped the wood into a cross. God met man on the Hill of Forgiveness. With divine strength, the Creator stooped to the anger of the created. With eternal love He allowed Himself to be wounded at the four extremities of the cross.

God paid for man with outstretched arms. He no longer hangs on the cross, but His arms are in the same position. Because of Him, we are forgiven in spite of ourselves. He receives the guilty. He welcomes the wounded.

None of us deserves this kind of forgiveness. It's a gift. Once you've received it, it's impossible to remain the same.

Jesus asks us to follow His example: "He did not retaliate when he was insulted, nor threaten revenge when he suffered. He left his case in the hands of God, who always judges fairly" (1 Peter 2:23, NLT). He says that forgiveness should become a way of life regardless of how unfair people may be to you:

> Get rid of all bitterness, rage, anger, harsh words, and slander, as well as all types of evil behavior. Instead, be kind to each other, tenderhearted, forgiving one another, just as God through Christ has forgiven you. (Ephesians 4:31–32, NLT)

We want rest. But it will cost us. The menu for rest lists many variations of humble pie. But if pride holds us hostage, we'll find that we are our own worst enemy. Maybe now is a good time for you to take a serious inventory of your life. Are there people you need to forgive? Do yourself a favor. Give them something they don't deserve but desperately need—the gift of forgiveness. It's a gift that once given offers something in return: your spirit gets a rest.

My football coach used to say, "Gentlemen, it takes fewer muscles to smile than to frown. We are going to need all your energy to win." That's sound advice whether you're trying to win at a game that lasts a couple of hours or a battle that lasts a lifetime. So don't waste your life on anger, fear, or regret. Clear the tension out of your heart through God's amazing power of forgiveness—and smile!

LIVING WITHIN
THE LIMITS

The Second Necessity

When you're raised in the country, hunting is just a natural part of growing up.

For years I enjoyed packing up my guns and some food and heading off into the woods. Even more than the hunting itself, I enjoyed the way those trips always seemed to deepen my relationship with friends as we hunted during the day and talked late into the night around the campfire. When an old friend recently invited me to relive some of those days, I couldn't pass up the chance.

For several weeks before the trip, I took the time to upgrade some of my equipment and the sight on my rifle. When the day came, I was ready for the hunt. What I wasn't ready for was what my close friend Tom shared with me the first night in camp.

I had always enjoyed the time I spent with Tom. He had become a leader in his church, and his warm and friendly manner had also taken him many steps along the path of business success. He had a nice wife, and while I knew they had traveled over some rocky terrain in their marriage, things now seemed to be stable and moving ahead smoothly. Tom's kids, two daughters and a son, were struggling in junior high and high school with the normal problems of peer pressure and acceptance.

Earlier, as we had driven into the mountains, I could tell that something big was eating away at Tom's heart. His normal effervescence was shrouded by an overwhelming inner ache. Normally Tom would attack problems with the same determination that had made him a success in business. Now I saw him wrestling with something that seemed to have knocked him to the mat for the count.

Silence has a way of speaking for itself. All day and on into the evening, Tom let his lack of words shout out his inner restlessness. Finally, around the first night's campfire, he opened up.

The scenario Tom painted was annoyingly familiar. I'd heard it many times before in many other people's lives. But the details seemed such a contrast to the life Tom and his wife lived and the beliefs they embraced.

His oldest daughter had become attached to a boy at school. Shortly after they started going together, they became sexually involved. Within two months, she was pregnant. Tom's wife discovered a packet from Planned Parenthood. When confronted with it, the girl admitted she had picked it up when she went to the clinic to find out if she was pregnant.

Countless parents through the years have faced this devastating news. Being a member of such a large fraternity of history, however, does not soften the severity of the blow to your heart when you discover it's your daughter.

Tom shared the humiliation he experienced when he realized that all of his teaching had been ignored. Years of spiritual training had been thrust aside. His stomach churned as he relived the emotional agony of knowing that the little girl he and his wife loved so much had made a choice that had seriously scarred her heart.

I'm frequently confronted with these problems in my work and have found that dwelling on the promiscuous act only makes matters worse. It also undermines a person's ability to focus on the greater concerns of rebuilding the girl's life and making good choices regarding the new life growing inside of her. I worship a God of forgiveness and wise solutions, and at that moment in our conversation I was intent on turning Tom toward hope and healing. I asked him what they had decided to do—would they keep the baby or make an adoption plan?

That's when he delivered the blow.

With the fire burning low, Tom paused for a long time before answering. And even when he spoke, he wouldn't look me in the eye.

"We considered the alternatives, Tim. Weighed them all." He took a deep breath. "We finally made an appointment with the abortion clinic. I took her down there myself."

I dropped the stick I'd been poking the coals with and stared at Tom. Except for the wind in the trees and the snapping of our fire, it was quiet for a long time. I couldn't believe this was the same man who for years had been so outspoken against abortion. He and his wife had even volunteered at a crisis pregnancy center in his city.

Heartsick, I pressed him about the decision. Tom then made a statement that captured the essence of his problem—and the problem many others have in entering into genuine rest.

In a mechanical voice, he said, "I know what I *believe,* Tim, but that's different from what I had to *do.* I had to make a decision that had the fewest consequences for the people involved."

Just by the way he said it, I could tell that my friend had rehearsed these lines over and over in his mind. And by the look in his eyes and the emptiness in his voice, I knew his words sounded as hollow to him as they did to me.

In one sweeping statement, Tom had articulated a major trend that is robbing so many homes of rest.

When Uncomfortable Circumstances
Push Aside Our Beliefs

Let me list a few of the ways I've seen people trying to live on both sides of the fence:

- A service manager is outspoken about his desire to be a deacon at his church but is even more outspoken in his use of coarse language at work to "motivate" his men.

- A mother never misses her weekly installments of the promiscuous trashy evening shows on television but preaches to her daughter about the questionable messages of rock music.

- An employee outfits his desk at home with supplies he requisitioned from work.

- A man goes on vacation with his family but makes one "business" call in order to deduct the entire trip on his income taxes.

- A mother reprimands her child for lying to her but consistently asks the same child to tell unwanted callers that she's "not home."

- A husband lectures his kids about their taste in movies but rents provocative DVDs for private viewing.

- A mom and dad drop the kids off at church while they slip away for some "needed time together" at a coffee shop.

A funny thing happened on the way to the twenty-first century. We decided that the concept of sin was something we should leave behind as confining and archaic. While we were busy locating the elusive self inside of us, we decided that all forms of guilt were bad and should be avoided at all costs. Since many sinful actions cause guilt, we found ourselves desperate to find relief from the pain. The only solution was to change the rules and redefine *wrong*.

Newsweek columnist Meg Greenfield had some interesting thoughts on this phenomenon in a piece titled, "Why Nothing Is 'Wrong' Anymore." In our society, she suggested, the word *wrong* has been taken out of "right and wrong." What's been substituted? How about "right and stupid"? Or "right and unconstitutional"? Or "right and emotionally ill"?[6]

Don't think her analysis of our cultural sickness stops outside the front door of the Christian community. On the contrary, it has come right inside and made itself at home within our ranks. Many Christians today would change the couplet to read, "right and what I *feel* is right." In other words, let's skip over those tough sections of the Bible that talk about God's hatred for adultery and divorce in favor of sections filled with more hope and compassion. I think of people like Alice, who read all the verses about not marrying a person who did not share her Christian convictions but married one anyway because "it can't be wrong when it feels so right." Their child is now suffering from the spiritual ambivalence that comes when a father is indifferent or antagonistic to the Christian faith of the mother.

I think of people like Chad, who met and married a woman on the same weekend his divorce came through because he *felt* God wanted him to—and that very weekend his former wife came looking for him to ask if he'd be willing to restore their relationship.

I think of people like Kyle, who volunteered his time at a crisis pregnancy center to give unborn children the right to life—but chose not to allow a pregnant daughter to live at home because of the negative effect it would have on his reputation.

Where does the epidemic of hypocrisy and shifting standards leave us? Without exception, it leads us to the wilderness of unrest. How can we return to the place where right is right and wrong is not excused on the basis of our feelings? Only by following a narrow way marked by an eternal Book—a pathway that offers freedom and rest by giving us the choice to live life within the standards of God's Word.

Throughout Scripture and down through the ages, those who have entered into God's rest have done so by making a conscious choice to stay within the protective fence of His standards. Put another way, the further we walk away from biblical guidelines, the closer we come to falling off the cliffs of anxiety, fear, worry, and unrest.

Back in 1967, a classmate that I later met in graduate school spent four harrowing months in Vietnam before being wounded and shipped home. One story he told taught me a lot about the urgency of staying within protective boundaries.

As the Vietnam War escalated, Mike knew that his chance of being drafted was high. And so he decided to enlist. It was a good thing, because two days later he received his draft notice. *At least,* he told himself, *I'm going to get a choice of what branch and what unit I'll be in.* Mike chose artillery because he figured that if he did have to go to Nam, at least he'd be behind the lines lobbing shells at the enemy from a safe distance. What he didn't know was that his choice would put him smack in the middle of some of the heaviest fighting of the war.

Following his training, Mike received orders to go overseas with a unit assigned to guard the perimeter of the Da Nang air base. On the long flight to Vietnam, the men congratulated themselves on their good fortune at being stationed so far from the front lines. And while this proved true for many of the men, the first thing Mike found waiting for him at the airfield was a packet with special orders. He was to immediately join a convoy that took his field piece and four men over treacherous territory to a Green Beret camp—right on the edge of no man's land.

The Special Forces stationed at this remote fire base were weapons experts, skilled in search and destroy missions and hand-to-hand combat. Mike and his gun crew found themselves the only regular army soldiers in the middle of this elite fighting corps. For nearly four months, Mike learned the lifesaving nature of boundaries—as two eight-foot barbed wire fences provided a sense of protection. For almost a hundred yards outside the outermost fence, all the grass and trees had been cleared. Buried land mines and other antipersonnel ordnance hidden in this open area provided further protection for those within the compound.

There were unmarked trails through the mines that the Green Berets would follow from memory as they came in and out from patrol. One afternoon, a man under Mike's command ventured gingerly across one of those trails to pick some fruit in the nearby jungle.

Besides an occasional mortar shell falling near the perimeter, there had been no direct enemy attack since they had taken up their station. In fact, it had been over a week since his gun battery had been called upon to provide supporting fire for one of the patrols. Even then it was for a unit near the limits of his range.

"Why can't we go outside the fence for a while?" one of his gunners had asked. "The Berets do it all the time. I've memorized the path through the mines by watching them." Lounging near their artillery piece, the rest of the crew watched as this man headed out of the compound toward the fresh fruit that had tempted all of them since their arrival.

Mike's friend had nearly reached the edge of the forest when they saw him stop suddenly and take a step back. He turned abruptly and began to run back toward the fence. That's when the sickening sound of machine-gun fire started to rip from the jungle. The young man collapsed immediately. He was dead before he hit the ground. In just moments, the quiet that had lasted for weeks was shattered by the scream of incoming mortar rounds. The attacking North Vietnamese Army troops poured out of the jungle like angry fire ants, many of them following the very route they had seen Mike's friend take through the minefield.

For over an hour the fighting was intense—and often hand-to-hand. At one point Mike ordered his artillery piece cranked down as low as possible, firing point-blank into the incoming troops. Somehow the men held their position. Mike and many others sustained severe wounds, but lived. Others weren't so fortunate.

As Mike related this story, he closed it with words that summarized a much greater principle in life: "Tim, you want to know why I don't fight God when it comes to areas He tells me in His Word to avoid? Because I've seen what can happen when you venture outside the fences of protection, and I don't want any part of it."

Whether we realize it or not, when we decide to walk away from God's Word and the clear boundaries it establishes for our lives, we are walking into no man's land. While the danger we face won't be bullets or mortar fire, the spiritual flames and arrows of an unseen Enemy can prove every bit as deadly. No piece of fruit, however tempting, is worth rendering ourselves defenseless and vulnerable by venturing outside the fence of God's Word.

The Gift of Guilt

We might never have thought of it this way before, but one of the greatest gifts God has given us is the ability to experience and feel guilt. While Freud and others have called it the "universal neurosis" and a destructive force in people's lives, guilt can actually be a means God uses to protect us. Like the nerve endings beneath our skin that cause us to draw back from a flame, guilt can alert us that we are getting too close to attitudes or actions that can do a lot of damage to us and the people we love.

I'm not saying that all guilt is good. Imaginary guilt, or guilt imposed on us by people wanting to control us, doesn't serve our best interests. Scripture tells us there is a sorrow that leads to death, but it also speaks of a godly sorrow that leads to repentance (see 2 Corinthians 7:9–10). It's this second aspect of guilt that we need to make our ally, not our enemy.

Guilt serves us spiritually the way fever serves us physically. When we get a fever, our bodies are telling us we have an infection somewhere inside of us. People who want to get better don't ignore their symptoms. Neither do they hate themselves because they're feeling sick. Nor do they simply take medications that mask their fever. Rather the negative feelings act as a physical reminder that the fence between sickness and health has been crossed. Wise treatment says to address the infection. The fever will go away when the infection is under control.

In the same way, guilt tells us that something is wrong with us emotionally or spiritually. It says in a clear way, "You're stepping outside the fence by making this decision…pursuing this relationship…avoiding this person…accepting this invitation…"

To use another analogy, guilt is like the oil light on your vehicle's instrument panel. When it comes on, it's saying, "Hey, friend, check your oil! You're headed for problems if you don't." You can choose to ignore this spiritual warning light. By repeatedly sinning, you may even sever the wires that connect it. But ultimately, the consequence of your sin will bring your life to a screeching halt.

As we close this chapter, let me make two suggestions that can help you grab hold of this crucial element of rest. The first has to do with the subtle difference between *beliefs* and *values*. The second has to do with the incredible impact living within the lines can have on your friends and loved ones.

Embracing God's Boundaries

For the past twenty years, our nation has been shifting from living according to *beliefs* to living according to *values*. Let's define the difference.

A belief system answers the question, "What is right and what is wrong?" A value system answers the question, "What am I going to do?" Beliefs form the foundation on which we anchor our lives and give us a clear standard to live by. Values, on the other hand, should be an outgrowth of our beliefs. Beliefs should represent absolutes; values should represent the actions we take based on those beliefs.

For the Christian, another aspect is thrown into the mix. Instead of simply asking, "What is right and what is wrong?" we have been given guidelines in God's Word that call us to ask, *"Because of my belief in Christ,* what is right and what is wrong?" Beliefs take their shape in that book that sits on our nightstand or that we carry to church—the Scriptures. Values are those actions that should flow out of the beliefs we form based on His Word—a recognition that we are the Lord's and our lives are not our own. With this in mind, let's move from the theoretical to the practical.

To ignore or explain away our beliefs and then insist that we still have "values" is like trying to wag a tail that is no longer attached to the dog. My friend Tom had an absolute understanding of and a firm belief in the sanctity of human life—until it inconvenienced him. Then he simply adjusted his values so that they were more comfortable to live with. He quit asking, "Based on the Scriptures, what is right and wrong?" and simply stuck with asking, "What should I do that will cause the least discomfort or inconvenience to me?" His values still had to have a base to stand on, only now, instead of resting on God's Word, they stood on shifting sand.

As a nation, we have dealt with difficult moral issues in much the same way my friend Tom dealt with his dilemma. Instead of holding firm to the bedrock biblical principles of right and wrong, we have simply changed our minds about whether something is right or wrong.

We used to be a nation largely opposed to gambling; today poker is a sport on ESPN. It's seldom if ever addressed from the pulpits, and most states sponsor lotteries. Intoxication was once frowned on; today most parents have resigned themselves that it's just a natural part of the teenage experience. Premarital sex was the exception in the past; now it's the rule. According to federal statistics, half of the women getting married during the 1960s had sex before marriage. Today, more than four out of five women getting married report that they've had at least one sexual experience.[7]

Of the 50 percent of women getting married in the 1960s who confessed to premarital sex, most of them would've admitted that their actions were wrong. On the other hand, if you polled the 80 percent of women getting married today who admit to having had premarital sex, few of them would say they had done anything wrong. The same goes for our young men. Most teenage boys don't feel the slightest twinge of guilt even when they engage in casual sex.

Once we left our belief system behind—what God's Word clearly says about right and wrong—society also began turning down the volume on our consciences. And therein lies the greatest threat to rest in our home: as we become more comfortable at having one standard for our spiritual destiny and another for our daily choices and actions, we complicate the task of parenting—and increase our personal level of restlessness.

Here's the bottom line regarding the element of rest: we need to align our actions with our beliefs. By doing that, we acknowledge that God has put a protective fence around our behavior. We honor Him, we honor our loved ones, and we honor ourselves by respecting it. If we try to explain away its existence, we're going to trip headlong into a world of hurt.

If we haven't already, we need to ask ourselves a difficult question that demands an honest answer: are there areas, actions, goals, relationships, or dreams in our lives that we know fall outside the boundary of God's Word? To whatever degree we have walked outside the fence to embrace these things—no matter how attractive the fruit—we are, to that degree, preventing ourselves from experiencing genuine rest.

God promised to lead Joshua and the ancient nation of Israel to a place of rest. But along with the promise came a warning: "Be strong and very courageous.... Do not turn from [the law] to the right or to the left, that you may be successful wherever you go" (Joshua 1:7).

In some cases, staying within the fence of God's Word is far more difficult on the front side of the decision than walking outside it—but our sleep will be sweeter and our life filled more fully with His calm. And that's not all. Our example of living life within the limits can lead others to find rest as well. Just as it did for one pastor several years ago.

Limits That Provide Lessons

He was the shepherd of a large congregation. One Sunday morning he preached a sermon on honesty at each of his church's three services. The next day, with his car in the shop, he chose to use the local bus to get to his office.

He stepped up into the bus and handed the driver a five-dollar bill. (This was a number of years ago when the phrase "Exact change, please" had not yet been coined by bus drivers.) The driver took the pastor's money and gave him his ticket and a handful of bills.

When the pastor got to his seat and went to put the change back in his wallet, he noticed that the driver had given him too much. For the duration of the bus trip, the pastor made every attempt to rationalize why he should keep the change. *Maybe God knows I needed some extra money this week… Maybe I could give this extra money to His service…*

But his conscience wouldn't let him off. On his way out the door, he stopped and handed the money to the driver. "I'm afraid you made a mistake," he said. "You've given me too much change."

The driver smiled. "There was no mistake, Pastor. I was at your church yesterday and heard you preach on honesty. When you handed me that five, I thought I'd see if you were as good at practicing as you are at preaching!"

As the bus idled at the stop, the driver continued. "You know, Sunday was the first time I agreed to go to church with my wife. I've always thought you guys were a bunch of phonies, but I guess there's more to it than that. I'll see you *next* Sunday."

"No fair! Entrapment!" some might shout today. Yet this bus driver saw in real life that the pastor's beliefs and actions corresponded—and it led him to take a closer look at Jesus Christ.

How about us? Are we experiencing the benefits of concrete beliefs and corresponding actions?

Husbands, like it or not, your wife is looking at you today and asking that question. Wives, it's being asked of you too. Parents, get ready to be tested if you haven't been already. Children can sniff out hypocrisy like a pet duck can sniff out popcorn. And while we may put on a great front for those who don't know us as well at work or at church, this is the age of 24/7 news coverage and no-holds-barred analysis. If what you say you believe isn't what you're living, you don't have to be a political candidate to have your inconsistency end up on YouTube.

We give our family and ourselves an incredible gift when we make the decision to live within God's limits. It opens the door to genuine rest in our lives, and perhaps even more importantly, it models the pathway to rest that others can follow as well.

AN ETERNAL
PERSPECTIVE

The Third Necessity

My wife and I always viewed our children's bedtime as the most critical time of their daily routine. (Getting up was critical time number two.) Before Mr. Sandman arrived to sprinkle sleep dust in their eyes, we liked to sprinkle some rest into their souls. Rest for their bodies prepared them for tomorrow, but rest for their souls prepared them for a lifetime. How we brought the daily clutter of events, emotions, and experiences to a conclusion had a big effect on how my children would view themselves and the world in which they were attempting to live.

Darcy and I were painfully aware that these moments of closeness were passing. As we watched our children outgrow favorite toys, favorite songs, and favorite pillows, we knew that they must soon outgrow this little bedtime ritual as well. Sooner than we expected, our children become too big to rock to sleep. So these special times of reflection and perspective could not be taken lightly. The calmness of spirit passed on to our children during these strategic moments at the end of their day would have to serve them in the darkest hours of their lives.

That's why I liked to use the final conversations of their day to emphasize the third necessity for genuine rest. It's the one that most affected their choices. If I could implant this one perspective in the deepest crevices of their young minds, I knew it could save them from making a lot of mistakes—and give their spirits a consistent sense of freedom.

Everything in life takes on a different perspective when weighed against eternity. Relationships, accomplishments, and disappointments all assume significant new meanings. It was essential that my children learn to factor in the eternal as they calculated the meaning of the various circumstances that blended together in their formula of life.

The purpose of all this is neither to spoil the joy of a victory nor to soften the seriousness of a defeat. Life is both temporal and eternal. The day-to-day events that bring wrinkles to our foreheads, smiles to our faces, or tears to our eyes have a right to an immediate response. Whether we skin our knees, wound our spirits, or break our hearts, the emotions of the moment need to be felt and properly processed. It would be wrong to deny them expression.

Winning the Little League championship calls for a celebration, and being cut from this year's cheerleading squad might require sackcloth and ashes. Nothing is gained by reminding your son that "as far as eternity goes, the outcome of the game is meaningless." Nor does the counsel that "when you're dead and gone, no one will remember who was on the cheerleading squad" do anything but demonstrate an appalling lack of sensitivity on our part.

An absurd preoccupation with the sweet by-and-by makes us of little value to hurting people living in the nasty here and now. Nonetheless, *we are eternal people.* Because we are, it would be equally absurd to ignore the obvious impact of our eternal nature. True, planet earth logs time in hours, minutes, and seconds. And the tombstones that checker the cemeteries of the world have two dates under each name. But it's easy to forget that time is only relevant to our physical bodies. The soul that shares the body lives beyond the tomb, and its eternal destination has a timely influence on our day-to-day perspective.

There's that word again. So much of the key to rest is wrapped up in our *perspective*. That's why seeing ourselves against an eternal backdrop is so critical. If forgiveness gives us the ability to love and if clear boundaries provide a crystallized purpose, an eternal perspective gives us hope. Again, that's the reason I like to throw the experiences of the day up against the infinite backdrop of God's plan. As we reviewed our children's day and noted the highlights as well as tried to give wise counsel about the low spots, we also tried to remind them of their eternal legacy. They needed to know that they aren't chance happenings on a planet with no purpose. Today was no accident. Tomorrow is part of forever.

The Security of the Eternal

I'm amazed how many people get tripped up on this issue. So many of the disappointments in people's lives come because they fail to factor in the eternal. Without a regular reminder that "this world is not my home; I'm just passing through," we find it hard to enjoy contentment. We are forced to evaluate everything happening to us by arbitrary and superficial standards. Self-worth becomes an issue of achievement and arbitrary physical standards. Satisfaction becomes an issue of acquisition. Without the eternal, I'm in competition with the best the world can bring against me rather the best that lies within me. If I'm not feeling pushed by the competition breathing down my neck, I'm feeling pulled by those who are way ahead of me.

Life without an eternal perspective trades living for longing, exchanges happiness for hurriedness, and gives up rest for restlessness. When this life is all we've got going for us, we're forced to grab all the gusto we can, as fast as we can.

But once upon a time, an eternal God decided to give rest to people. He issued an invitation to slow down and last longer. The price tag was high, but the end result was worth it for Him. He gave up something in order for us to win. He knew that living would first require dying but that death would be the gateway to eternal life.

So the God who once slept in a manger climbed up on a cross. He paid the price for our inner rest. He took the shame, the guilt, and the punishment for our sins. He took care of the one problem all people share in common—our lost condition—which is also the one problem we cannot solve on our own.

But His Word makes it clear that dying wasn't enough. On Sunday morning, when the stone that sealed Jesus in His crypt was supernaturally rolled back, the morning light crept across the floor and up the ledge to a pile of grave clothes. The cloths that had concealed His death face had been carefully folded and placed where His lifeless head once lay.

Jesus vacated the grave in order to invade our hearts. Without the resurrection of Christ, there is only man-made hope. When Paul addressed this issue, he recognized how genuine hope pivots on the certainty that Christ deserted the grave:

> If only for this life we have hope in Christ, we are to be
> pitied more than all men. (1 Corinthians 15:19)

The message of the cross takes us beyond this life to eternal life. Those who embrace this truth are given the assurance that life on earth is just the beginning—a dress rehearsal.

The best is yet to come.

An Eternal Perspective Changes the Way We View People

If the best is yet to come, then we need to be careful about how we treat people. An eternal perspective reminds us that nothing on earth is more important than human beings. It's more than an issue of the sanctity of life. It's the reality that every person who walks on planet earth embodies a spirit that will live forever. No other created thing can make that claim. Without a regular reminder that we are eternal, we could easily be drawn into the snare of prioritizing things over people. It's an easy trap to fall into—and has a lot to do with the volatile nature of relationships.

Relationships are risky. They have the power to make us or break us at a moment's notice. Even the most secure and balanced person is affected. Relationships become a guarded game of one-upmanship and keeping the other guy off balance. We protect our intimate associations and are careful not to let too many people get close to us.

Things, on the other hand, seem more secure and become an attractive substitute for intimacy. They reward our egos and placate our consciences. We can surround ourselves with trophies. We can entertain ourselves to death with expensive toys. We can even be applauded for community service that raises money for faceless people living on the wrong side of the tracks. As long as we don't have to personally hold the cup of cold water as they're drinking from it, we're fine.

We can build a financial empire at the expense of our families and soothe our guilty spirits with rationalizations. "It's good for the economy." "It gave a lot of people jobs." "It provided my family with a better standard of living." There is no end to the ways we attempt to justify our love affairs with things. But the fact is, we were designed to find completion in relationships, not in material possessions.

When we allow anything to undermine our responsibilities to others, we find a growing emptiness in our hearts. That's because, like it or not, we can't make it without relationships.

What we need to do is make choices that don't jeopardize eternal relationships for temporary rewards. An eternal perspective helps us do that. Those who recognize that people are more important than personal gain or personal satisfaction have a better chance of maintaining a rested spirit. It also helps them stay married and effectively prepare their children for true greatness. They run their daily decisions through a grid that would never allow something that lasts for a moment (or even a lifetime) to take priority over a person who lasts forever.

My wife and I cling to a simple decision-making principle, an elementary rule of thumb that has kept us from veering off course again and again. Bob Kraning, a popular speaker from Southern California, shared this principle. It's some of the best counsel I've ever received, and it's given Darcy and me a deep-seated confidence when facing tough choices about our kids, our friends, and each other. The principle is simply this:

Never sacrifice the permanent on the altar of the immediate.

There are few guarantees in life, but I can guarantee you that making choices according to this principle can keep you from neglecting the priority of people. It all hinges on an eternal perspective.

An Eternal Perspective Changes the Way We View Love

Knowing there's more to life than life on earth changes the way we view love. It can't be taken lightly. The people who represent the crucial relationships in our lives must be constantly viewed according to their eternal potential. Their destiny is contingent on their response to God's work on the cross. I must take care, therefore, never to undermine their attitude toward God by taking a passive attitude toward my commitments to them.

Love is eternal. Although marriage vows are confined to time, love isn't. Although death will someday separate me from my children, we will meet again in heaven. Friends who embrace Christ for their salvation need to be viewed as *eternal* friends.

Years ago I picked up a collection of the works of Edgar Allan Poe and read some of the poems about love to my daughter, Karis, who was six at the time. My favorite turned out to be her favorite too: "Annabel Lee." She enjoyed it so much that she asked me to help her commit it to memory. In the days that followed, I reviewed it with her until she had it word perfect.

If you recall the poem, Annabel Lee was a young girl Poe loved. But she came down with pneumonia and died before they were able to be married. The poem speaks of a love that cannot be consumed by death:

It was many and many a year ago,
    In a kingdom by the sea,
That a maiden there lived whom you may know
    By the name of Annabel Lee;
And this maiden she lived with no other thought
    Than to love and be loved by me.

I was a child and she was a child,
    In this kingdom by the sea,
But we loved with a love that was more than love,
    I and my Annabel Lee;
With a love that the winged seraphs of heaven
    Coveted her and me.

And this was the reason that, long ago,
    In this kingdom by the sea,
A wind blew out of a cloud, chilling
    My beautiful Annabel Lee;
So that her highborn kinsmen came
    And bore her away from me,
To shut her up in a sepulcher
    In this kingdom by the sea.

The angels, not half so happy in heaven,
    Went envying her and me;
Yes! that was the reason (as all men know,
    In this kingdom by the sea)
That the wind came out of the cloud by night,
    Chilling and killing my Annabel Lee.

But our love it was stronger by far than the love
    Of those who were older than we,
    Of many far wiser than we;
And neither the angels in heaven above,
    Nor the demons down under the sea,
Can ever dissever my soul from the soul
    Of the beautiful Annabel Lee:

For the moon never beams without bringing me dreams
    Of the beautiful Annabel Lee;
And the stars never rise, but I feel the bright eyes
    Of the beautiful Annabel Lee;
And so, all the night-tide, I lie down by the side
Of my darling—my darling—my life and my bride,
    In her sepulcher there by the sea,
    In her tomb by the sounding sea.[8]

After reading the poem together, Karis and I had one of the best conversations about time and eternity we'd ever had. It was an opportunity to review with her again the truth that *love isn't confined to time.* I wanted her to see the people she loves from an eternal perspective. That understanding can medicate her heart when it gets broken. When she loses someone she dearly loves, there will still be reason to smile.

My mother died when I was thirty-four. I could go into a moving eulogy about what a great woman she was, but she wouldn't have preferred that. Mom made a quiet yet clear statement about God in the way she loved my father, loved us kids, and cared for people. For her, human legacies were the only kind worth leaving.

At her funeral some well-meaning people tried to comfort me with worn-out clichés. The bromide most frequently whispered in my ear was "Time heals all wounds." It's now been several decades since we buried Mom, and the pain of missing her is as compelling today as it was when I watched them lower her casket into the ground. Time *doesn't* necessarily heal all wounds. But when you love someone, it doesn't have to! The pain of missing Mom is a reminder of how special she was. It's a pain that puts a smile on my face.

An Eternal Perspective Changes the Way We View Death

Maintaining an eternal perspective helps us avoid a morbid preoccupation with death. Death doesn't have to loom on the horizon of life as a vicious thief. It can be accepted in a healthy way as one of the necessary parts of life's formula.

My mother was diagnosed as terminally ill with cancer a few months before she died. The hospice program she was confined to did a lot to help her and my family walk more effectively through the "valley of the shadow of death." I was reading one of their brochures in her room one day. Life, it said, is a process made up of three parts: you are born, you live, and you die. Healthy people are those who learn to accept death as a part of life.

That's fine, I thought, *except you forgot something. You're born, you live, you die, and then you live forever!* That's why King David referred to it as the "valley of the *shadow* of death" and not the "valley of death" (Psalm 23:4).

Shadows can't hurt me. What cast the shadow can. But God challenged death to a duel, and death chose a cross as its weapon. God fired back with an empty grave. He defeated death when He walked out of its grip into the light of a beautiful Sunday morning. For those who trust in this truth, it's eternally Sunday. That's why we can respond to the shadows of death that cross our path with the words of David: "I will fear no evil" (Psalm 23:4).

The job description of the Christian life says we must be prepared to die at a moment's notice. God has taken the sting out of this process through the cross.

And once we are prepared to die, we are free to live.

An Eternal Perspective Changes the Way We View Aging

Have you ever noticed how the gravitational pull of the earth increases once you hit thirty? It's amazing how these bodies that once climbed mountains while barely breaking a sweat suddenly need jump-starting to get us from the dinner table to the recliner. I'm not ready to roll over and die, but I do find that the process of staying in shape and feeling healthy requires deliberate daily choices. It's the human dilemma called "the end doesn't justify the jeans."

I like to get up every morning and run. Correction: I like to get up every morning; I choose to run. It's the lesser of the evils that face me as I move my way into the uncharted regions of middle age. I can let myself go to seed (which sounds like a lot more fun), or I can try to make the last half of my life as free of health problems as possible. That's why I get up and run.

There's a phenomenon in running called hitting the wall. It's the invisible barrier that suddenly slows you down and tells you to quit. It's usually waiting for me at the corner of my property. I have to give myself quite a sermon to get past the first few hundred yards. After that, the next few miles come more easily.

I'm glad I don't have to determine my value in life by how well I keep up with the starving models waltzing down the fashion runways of Madison Avenue and Milan. Realizing that I'm eternal has taken the threat out of aging. Planet earth possesses no fountain of youth, so I do the best I can with the health I have and accept, without threat (and too much whining), the inevitable effects of time.

I'll take it one step further: I'm convinced that an eternal perspective is the only thing that can give us the ability to actually *look forward* to growing old. Sure, there are liabilities. That's obvious. But there are assets that can offset them. Maturity steps in where youth steps out. Knowledge makes way for wisdom. Time becomes the valuable commodity it should have been from the beginning. And relationships become our life.

I should also mention that you are finally awarded offspring you actually get along with—grandchildren. The reason grandparents bond so well with their grandchildren is because they both share a common point of frustration.

Regardless, it isn't so bad growing old when you know that death isn't a period at the end of your life but a comma separating the good from the best.

An Eternal Perspective Changes the Way We View Time

Time is a commodity—a fixed number of days consumed but not replenished. It is the constant ticking on our wrist or the numbers that silently stare at us from our alarm clock during a sleepless night. We block it into neat little days, stack them on top of each other, and call them months. We attach a pretty picture to the stack and package it as a calendar. But it's always moving. Racing forward. Ready or not, there it goes.

Time is a *process*. It's a homemade growth chart penciled on the doorjamb of the laundry room. It's boxes of neatly folded baby clothes stored in the attic. It's yearbooks with personal handwritten notes from people you don't remember. It's when you no longer care whether you win or lose but how you play the game.

Time is an *effect*. "Gee, Daddy, your hair is getting a lot grayer." "This belt's too small!" "I set out to do thirty push-ups but couldn't remember what number I was on." It's when you no longer care whether you win or lose but *if* you can play the game.

How we view our time has everything to do with our ability to enjoy genuine rest. An eternal perspective helps us to see time as a gift to be given to others, a precious investment in people who will live forever.

Perhaps you've run across the following story of a father and son who took two different views toward the proper use of time. They had the same last name and some similar physical characteristics, but other than that they were as different as night and day.

They farmed a little piece of land, and a couple times a year they would set out with their wagon filled with vegetables for the market in a nearby city. The father took the first turn at leading the ox, setting a modest pace, as his son sat fidgeting on the seat of the cart.

"Dad, we need to hurry so we can make it to town tonight. We've got to be in position to set up early enough to get the best prices."

"Don't worry, Son. We'll get there soon enough." After an hour and a half of watching his father casually walking beside the beast, the younger man insisted on taking his turn at leading. The father laid down on the seat to take a nap as the son started poking the ox with a stick and harassing him to pick up his gait. The father peered out from under his hat at his impatient boy.

"Take your time, Son. You'll last longer."

The determined boy just shook his head in disgust. He swatted the ox's back with a vengeance.

Several hours later the father sat up and stretched.

"Look, Son, my brother's house. Pull in so I can visit him. We live so close but see each other so little."

"Father, we don't have time!"

"What do you mean? All we have is time. That's why I want to use some of it talking to him."

The two men visited and laughed while the son paced. After an hour, the father and son were back on the road. The father was leading when they came to a fork in the road. He nudged the ox to the right.

"The path to the left is quicker!"

"But this way is prettier."

"Have you no respect for time?"

"I certainly do. That's why I like to spend it looking at beautiful things."

The young man pulled his hat down over his eyes, crossed his arms, sat back in the seat, and tapped his nervous foot against the harness. He was so busy fuming inside that he failed to see the beautiful garden of flowers that blanketed both sides of the path.

Toward dark, the father pulled over the wagon and started to unharness the ox for the night. The son didn't hide his anger.

"This is the last time I'll make this trip with you! If we had followed my plan, we would've been there by now. We could have been set up for tomorrow's buyers and been sold out by noon. You're more interested in flowers than in making money!"

"Why, that's the nicest thing you've ever said to me!"

With that statement, the father found a comfortable spot to lie down and was quickly asleep.

At dawn the son had the ox harnessed and his sleepy father in the seat. After an hour or so they came upon a man whose wagon was stuck in a ditch.

"Let's help him, Son."

"And lose more time?"

"Nonsense. You may find yourself in a ditch someday."

They helped the man out and then started back on the path. It was a little after eight o'clock. Up ahead a flash of lightning crossed the sky, thunder rolled in the distance, and the skies turned black.

"Looks like the city is getting quite a storm."

"If we had been there, enough of our produce would've sold by now that we wouldn't have to worry about the storm."

"Take your time, Son. You'll last longer."

It wasn't until late in the afternoon when they reached the bluff overlooking the city. They both stared down at it for a long time without speaking. Finally the son looked at the father.

"I see what you mean, Dad."

And they both turned their cart around and walked away from what had once been the city of Hiroshima.

SERVING WHILE SUFFERING

The Fourth Necessity

Millions of Americans start their day the same way. Their rooster is a favorite disc jockey or radio talk-show host jarring them awake while it's still dark outside.

Before their eyes can focus, their minds are already rifling through the to-dos of appointments, errands, chores, and projects that will be crammed into the handful of waking hours they're given that day.

If they're conscientious about how good they'll look in their casket after their heart attack, they may disappear around the block on their morning jog, grunt on an Ab Lounge, or shake and bake with some pilates maven on fast-forward.

With spouse and children competing for sinks, showers, blow-dryers, makeup, and at times even the same clothes, they manage to rinse off the night, dress, nuke a cup of coffee, and take a few bites of a breakfast that comes from a box via the toaster. Quick kisses are exchanged as family members race for the first stop on their busy schedules.

School buses, bicycles, skateboards, and carpools dispatch the kids as husband and wife gingerly open the doors of their separate cars—

careful not to drop their briefcases or tilt their coffee mugs too far. Biodegradable wrappers from previous trips to McDonald's exhale from Mom's SUV as she climbs in. While she's trying to dislodge the Happy Meal toy out of the crease in her driver's seat, Dad is scrolling through his iPhone so he can skim his e-mail during the drive to work. Husband and wife blow each other a kiss from opposite ends of the garage as the garage door lifts up and out of their way. That's when the grand marshal of the rat race gives his inaudible command: "Start your engines!"

Thousands of cars from one community merge with thousands of cars from another suburb on the eight-lane dragstrips that link bedroom with boardroom. It's the human race running in the human race.

The freeway has to be one of the most vivid illustrations of modern life imaginable. It can, at any given moment, express the heart and soul of a culture because it has, at any given moment, a complete representation of all strata of people.

The freeway is no respecter of persons. It doesn't discriminate according to age, gender, race, religion, or net worth. It's an asphalt artery carrying the rich and poor, the old and young, the winners and losers, the brazen and beaten. It's a collection of people trying to keep in line with the posted speed limit and still arrive at their next opportunity in life a little sooner. And like it or not, the speed of life the freeway represents is here to stay.

But there is a category of people on the freeway who do not represent the rank and file of life. Though these people would *like* to be a part of the mainstream, factors beyond their control hold them back. You notice them out of your peripheral vision as you speed by. Some of them are broken down on the shoulder of the freeway. Others wait anxiously by emergency call boxes.

Who are these people who have been shoved out of life's mainstream? They are the people around us who suffer. I've observed four types of sufferers stalled alongside the freeways of life. I call them the Bewildered, the Badgered, the Broken, and the Battered. Although their frustrations may have little in common, the effect of their frustrations on their sense of rest and calm is the same.

I've noticed a couple things about people who suffer. First, of all the deterrents to experiencing genuine rest, nothing can drain it away faster than suffering. Second, suffering people who are willing to pursue rest in their lives often enjoy *a richer and better degree of rest* than those who rest without suffering.

If you'll allow me to carry this analogy of a freeway a bit further, I'm sure you'll see my point.

Those Who Are Bewildered

A few years ago, the *Oregonian* carried the tragic account of an elderly couple from British Columbia who became disoriented while driving their motor home through Portland. They had a reservation at a local hotel but couldn't seem to locate it in the city's maze of bridges, ramps, and crisscrossing freeways. An unidentified man apparently saw them on the shoulder of a road consulting a city map. He pulled his car over and asked if he could help.

Perhaps the older lady, who was driving, couldn't understand his directions. That was why the man evidently suggested that the bewildered couple simply follow his car and he would lead them to their destination. It sounded like such a good idea. But something went wrong.

In her anxiety to keep up with the man's car, the woman failed to negotiate a turn and plunged the vehicle through a guardrail. The motor home flipped in the air and crashed upside down on the freeway some forty feet below. The woman died instantly; the man, en route to the hospital. The would-be guide slammed on his brakes, observed the carnage below, and then sped away before police could arrive on the scene.

We've all found ourselves disoriented from time to time.

Getting lost on the freeways of contemporary culture isn't that hard to do. With our rush-hour lifestyles and passing-lane mentalities, it's usually just a matter of time before we find ourselves moving with the flow…but not sure where we are.

Sometimes it's a case of not knowing where we're going. But I think that's usually the exception. Most often we know where we want to be in life; we're just not quite sure how to *get* there. And we're certain we don't want to be where we are.

In my line of work, I meet a lot of people who are confused. They're confused because people keep changing the rules. They're confused because they've been handed inaccurate road maps through life. They're confused because "reliable" people keep giving them wrong directions.

They may believe the truth of the Bible, but they've been given so much conflicting counsel that they've lost all sense of direction. *Rest?* It's out of the question, as anyone who has ever found himself lost or disoriented for any length of time will quickly agree.

Some three thousand years ago, Isaiah warned us of the highwaymen who control us by keeping us confused.

> Woe to those who call evil good, and good evil;
>> Who substitute darkness for light and light for
>> darkness;
>> Who substitute bitter for sweet, and sweet for
>> bitter!
> Woe to those who are wise in their own eyes
>> And clever in their own sight! (Isaiah 5:20–21, NASB)

Some good people get turned around on their way to contentment. Here are just a few of the wrong directions and misplaced road signs that send us veering off course:

- ◆ "There is no way that God ever intended for any of His children to be poor or sick."
- ◆ "Success is the only accurate way of measuring your true worth."

- ◆ "The top rung of the corporate ladder is the only one worth pursuing."
- ◆ "Don't let your family rob you of your big opportunity."
- ◆ "There are some sins your spouse can commit that are simply unforgivable."
- ◆ "You don't have to wait until you're making more money to enjoy your dream home now."

Most people succumb to these confusing signals because they stop submitting to the only road map that is universally reliable for traveling through life—the Bible. I think that can happen even if you still believe in God. All you have to do is stop depending on His daily guidance.

Although I believe in taking individual responsibility for one's actions, I can't help but feel that some of these folks who have lost their way are victims. They listened to the eloquent and well-dressed charlatans who maintain such an effective grip on this generation. Before these people knew it, they had been misled.

I know their plight. I've been misled. I've been confused. You have every confidence that you're doing well, heading in the right direction; then you look around and realize you're way off course. Until you find your way back to the right freeway, your life is filled with restless frustration.

Those Who Are Badgered

It's never happened to me, but I've seen it happen to others. Some guy with a chip on his shoulder gets in his car under the illusion that the government built the entire freeway system for his private use. He heads up the on-ramp and proceeds to claim ownership of all four lanes through the twenty-first-century art of auto intimidation.

He's angry. But the object of his anger isn't there to kick around, so he takes it out on other people. As long as there are people, there will be bullies. And unchecked bullies can destroy a lot of lives before someone brings them under control.

I've seen people forced to swerve into traffic to avoid them. I've seen the bullies slow down to give a senior citizen or some new teen driver a piece of their angry mind. I've seen the road hogs threaten a mother with a carload of kids. You want to do something, but you're often helpless.

Does this sound familiar? Have you made the connection between being badgered on the freeway and being badgered in your everyday life?

Maybe it's the neighborhood bully who keeps intimidating your kid while his father cheers him on.

Maybe it's the church gossip who won't let your past lie at the foot of the cross where you left it.

Maybe it's the tape of your mother's voice that plays over and over inside your head saying, "You'll never amount to anything."

Maybe it's the former spouse who is committed to destroying your new marriage.

Maybe it's the wayward son who keeps dragging you from the principal's office to juvenile court.

Maybe you're the qualified employee who deserves a promotion but is passed up because your manager wants her personal favorite or yes-man to have the position.

It doesn't take much badgering before you start to feel helpless. At that point, a rested spirit is as far from your mind as it can be.

The things (or people) that badger our lives don't have to be bigger, stronger, or more influential than us. They just have to be persistent.

A United States postal worker learned this in an unfortunate way. It seems that he was severely bitten by a dog belonging to a lonely and angry lady. Because of the extent of his wounds, the law required that the dog be destroyed. That was when the undeclared war began.

The lady's heart filled with rage. She decided that if she couldn't have her dog, then this man and his family would not have another day's rest as long as she lived. She called him at all hours of the night. Whoever answered the phone would be treated to an unsolicited tirade accented with shrill obscenities. It didn't matter whether it was his youngest child or his wife, the message was the same.

Naturally the postal worker changed his phone number. She found out what it was. He got an unlisted number. Her network of spies found that number. When she couldn't get him through the telephone, she used an even better form of communication—the gossip chains. She passed lies that couldn't help but discredit the man as a father and a government worker.

The man was forced to put his house up for sale and relocate in order to get peace. Before that happened, a judge of the court said enough is enough. He made it clear to the lady that even though she was over seventy years old, he would not hesitate to incarcerate her (without a phone) if she didn't bring this behavior to a halt. She called the judge's bluff, and he played his hand. He sent her to jail for thirty days. It's hard to believe, but she even tried the same trick from the phone at the jail.

What do you do when the only thing keeping someone alive is the joy he or she receives from hating you? How can you find rest when restlessness stalks you and hounds you every waking moment of your day?

Those Who Are Broken

Our urban culture is directly responsible for the traffic reporter. People in a hurry listen to them religiously. They warn us where the major traffic arteries have become snarled. They suggest alternative routes and escape options that will save us time. They keep our impatient spirits from exploding.

The primary problem they report is stalled or stranded vehicles. We've all experienced the frustration that builds inside when we sit in the middle of a bottleneck caused by a motorist with a flat tire or an overheated radiator. It burns us to think one guy could hold up so many people.

Some people's cars break down because they fail to maintain them. We think we're justified in ignoring them because they're probably getting what they asked for. But cars are machines, and even the best maintained machine will break down occasionally. Cars fresh off the showroom floor or straight from the mechanic's garage have failed in traffic. But when the average person is inconvenienced by them, he finds it hard to be patient. His emotions go in one of two directions. He's either annoyed that he's been held up, or he's glad that it happened to somebody else and not him.

There is a whole group of people stranded on the side of life's road who receive a similar response from people in the fast lane. For these people the inequities of life cause them to be the true sufferers.

The obvious members of this category are the physically handicapped. The wheelchair user, the blind, and the deaf have so much to offer but are often denied by a system that takes survival of the fittest to a ridiculous extreme. Because these examples are the extreme forms of physical handicap, we tend to think of them first. But there are a host of other sufferers stranded on the shoulder of the fast lane. Arthritics, those who suffer from cluster headaches or PMS, terminally ill patients, and those with speech impediments are just a few examples of those who are forced to live in a society that isn't very sympathetic to their problems.

Two other groups of people can find themselves sidelined simply because they are the "wrong" age. Children and senior citizens do not fit very well into our hurried lifestyle. When society doesn't want to accommodate them, they're often forced over to the shoulder, where they watch life rush by without them. The personal touch they desperately need is often a subcontracted out to strangers.

If you feel like you are one of these broken people, true rest is probably hard to come by.

Those Who Are Battered

One of the most terrifying experiences of life is to be involved in a car accident. At the instant of impact, lives can be permanently changed. Some accidents are nobody's fault. The damages may be severe, but the fact that it was unavoidable and no one was to blame doesn't necessarily make coping that much easier.

But what about those collisions that were the result of someone else's irresponsibility? They cut the heart out of your joy. They cause suffering that sometimes plagues you for life.

Then there are those other crashes. Terrible, silent collisions that never show up in the newspaper's accident reports. Battered men and women who face staggering emotional pain. Victims who must learn to live with a permanently injured life.

- The father who comes home to a full house but an empty bedroom. His wife didn't say where she was going, just that she would never be back.

- The parents who find their daughter's body next to a suicide note.

- The fifty-year-old employee who faithfully served his company but is out of a job because the company that purchased his company has decided to eliminate an entire level of management.

Sometimes the only mistake you made was being born into the wrong family. But that single unfortunate dilemma can cost you forever.

Take Edwin Thomas for instance. Edwin Thomas Booth, that is. At age fifteen he debuted on the stage playing Tressel to his father's Richard III. Within a few short years he was playing the lead in Shakespearean tragedies throughout the United States and Europe. He was the Laurence Olivier and Kenneth Branagh of his time. He brought a spirit to tragedy that put him in a class by himself.

Edwin had a younger brother, John, who was also an actor. Although he could not compare with his older brother, John did give a memo-rable interpretation of Marc Antony in the 1864 production of *Julius Caesar* by the Winter Garden Theatre in New York. Two years later, he performed his last role in a theater when he jumped from the box of a bloodied President Lincoln to the stage of Ford's Theatre. John Wilkes Booth met the end he deserved. But his murderous life placed a stigma over the life of his brother, Edwin.

An invisible asterisk now stood beside Edwin's name in the minds of people. He was no longer Edwin Booth, the consummate tragedian, but Edwin Booth, the brother of the assassin. He withdrew from the stage for a while to ponder the question "Why?" Edwin Booth's life was a tragic accident simply because of his last name. Sensationalists wouldn't let him separate himself from his brother's crime.

It is interesting to note that Edwin Booth carried a letter with him that could have vindicated him from the sibling attachment to his brother. It was a letter from General Adam Badeau, chief secre-tary to General Ulysses S. Grant, thanking him for a singular act of bravery. It seems that while Edwin was waiting for a train on the plat-form at Jersey City, a coach he was about to board bolted forward. He turned in time to see that a young man had slipped from the edge of the pressing crowd into the path of the oncoming train. Without thinking, Edwin raced to the edge of the platform and, linking his leg around a railing, grabbed the fellow by the collar. The grateful young man recognized him, but Edwin didn't recognize the young man. It wasn't until he received the letter of thanks that he learned the young man was Robert Todd Lincoln, the son of his brother's future victim.[9]

Tragedy wrings rest from our spirits. It did for Edwin Booth, and maybe it has for you. You may be bewildered, badgered, broken, or bat-tered. If you are, then you need the message that makes up the fourth principle of genuine rest.

The Power of Serving While Suffering

Suffering can cause us to turn our backs on the first three necessities for rest. It challenges our willingness to forgive; it tempts us to rationalize our wrong behavior; it so absorbs us that it's difficult to see past today. But the fourth necessity for rest can counter the effects of suffering. I use as my defense the one person "who has been tempted in all things as we are, yet without sin" (Hebrews 4:15, NASB).

Jesus was bewildered. God bewildered? The God side of the God-Man was never bewildered, but the humanity of Jesus felt the frustration of having to deal with inconsistent disciples, hypocritical religious leaders, and a divine plan to save man that required His impending death.

Jesus was badgered. From the outset of His ministry, Jesus was the object of public scorn. The religious leaders who should have welcomed Him with open arms led the chants against Him.

Jesus was broken. The Man of Sorrows broke down in a quiet corner of a city park. The blood that seeped from His sweat glands while He hung on the cross hinted at the extent of His anguish.

Jesus was battered. Sin, death, and Satan attacked Him at the cross. The holes they drove into His hands and feet and the spear wound in His side were only outward signs of an internal hurt. The God of Abraham, Isaac, and Jacob came to give His life for His enemies. He did it so that they could become His friends.

There are two actions Jesus took to counter the effects of the restless and ruthless world He came to save. They're the same solutions that can help bring rest back to your suffering spirit.

The Solution of Acceptance

When an individual finds himself having to endure some discomfort or severe suffering, it's easy for him to go to one of two extremes. He either denies that it could actually be happening to him, or he assumes that

God is going to intervene in some supernatural way and make the pain go away.

God is a God of miracles. He performs them all the time. But there is a difference between a God of miracles and a God of *magic*. Miracles are done for His glory; magic is performed for our entertainment. The normal human response to suffering is a heartfelt plea to take the pain away. But God isn't required to do it, nor is it His usual way of handling our problems.

To deny the reality of our suffering is unhealthy. Imagine that your company lays you off at age fifty from a high-paying job and you can't get work anywhere because you're too old. It might be tempting to fantasize that you're going to wake up one morning and find that they're inviting you back to head the company. But it's as unlikely that you'll be able to enjoy inner rest with that attitude as it is that they'll invite you back.

You might find out that you have a debilitating disease. God could miraculously heal you, but what if He chooses not to?

You could be living with an alcoholic. You could deny that he is an alcoholic. You could believe that God is going to intervene and take away his craving for alcohol. You can choose to believe that real-life stories have fairy-tale endings. But a more biblical approach is to *accept* the obvious and the inevitable. Honesty with yourself is the best prerequisite to being honest with the alcoholic.

Jesus knew that He was heading for a cross. During His three-year public ministry, He alluded several times to His ultimate destiny. But as He got closer, the human nature that hurts and feels rejection surfaced. At one point He fell on His face, pleading with His Father to see if there was any way that "this cup [could] pass" from Him (see Matthew 26:39, NASB). He loved lost people and was committed to obeying His Father, but like any person with human feelings, He wanted to avoid the excruciating suffering that was awaiting Him on the cross.

An interesting thing happened once Jesus accepted the inevitable.

He got up off the ground, wiped the tears and dirt from His face, and went to face His fate. Maybe contrasting Him with the disciples will help you see the power He derived from accepting the obvious.

You recall that when Jesus went to the garden to pray, He requested that His disciples get together and pray on His behalf. They'd had a busy day. It was late. The physical won out over the spiritual, and they fell asleep. Meanwhile Jesus, who'd had an even tougher day, agonized in prayer over the impending battle for the souls of men. When He finally finished praying and had accepted what was to come, He calmly awakened the sleeping disciples and prepared them for the mob that was at that very moment making its way through the garden to arrest Him. At that point, the disciples panicked. Peter made a feeble attempt at defending Jesus and then ran with the rest of them to the dark corners and back streets of Jerusalem. Throughout the entire trial, flogging, ridicule, and crucifixion, Christ displayed a quiet, determined calm. It was rooted in His acceptance of the circumstances and His confidence in His Father's plan.

The Solution of Serving

No more mobs trying to get near enough to touch the edge of His garments. No more afternoon sermons on the hills overlooking the Sea of Galilee. No more parades with palm branches, laughing children, and applauding adults. Just a cross-shaped gallows, some nails, a hammer, some indifferent executioners, and the salvation of the human race.

I find it hard to understand, but at the one time in Jesus's earthly ministry when He needed to be concentrating on His own problems, He chose to accommodate the needs of others. In His example we find a key necessity for a rested heart. Jesus knew that *rest doesn't come in serving yourself but in serving others.* He knew that His own pain could never be an excuse for ignoring the pain of others.

He looked down from the cross and saw the middle-aged woman who had, as a teenager, submitted to the God she loved and offered her womb as an incubator for the King of kings. Mary was graying now. With all that had transpired in the past few days, she looked beaten. He spoke to the one disciple He was sure would be responsible enough to fulfill His request. He asked John to make certain that she was cared for.

Jesus hung between social scum. He was the lily floating in the cesspool. But He knew that He was dying to give hope to the very men with whom He was being crucified. At first both thieves mocked Him. But ultimately the one asked Him for help. Jesus turned His tired and bloody head far enough to catch the man's eyes. He gave him a promise and a confidence that they would soon be in paradise together. That man became the first convert of the crucified Lord. (Indeed, the last shall be first.)

It's hard to understand why people of every culture maintain such a morbid fascination with death. But they do. On that Friday morning when they hammered Jesus to the cross, quite a crowd was taking it all in. Many of them hurled insults at Him and cracked jokes about His claims to deity. Along with them was a collection of soldiers who had long since turned cynical about the issue of meaningful life. For them it was just another execution. Just three more useless criminals. Well, not completely useless. Their shoes and coats were still good. They wouldn't be needing them where *they* were going. The real nice one, the one taken off Jesus, supplied an interesting distraction. It was too good to tear apart and divide equally. It was worth gambling over.

While people watched, men laughed, and soldiers wagered, Jesus turned His heart toward heaven and prayed a prayer on their behalf. He said, "Father, forgive them. They haven't a clue about what they're doing" (Luke 23:34, my paraphrase).

Jesus found rest in accepting the cross and serving others. His example is vital to the suffering heart looking for rest. He said, "If anyone wishes to come after Me, he must deny himself, and take up his cross and follow Me" (Mark 8:34, NASB). He knew that we can't necessarily change the behavior of others, but we can control our attitudes.

He said, "Love your enemies and pray for those who persecute you" (Matthew 5:44, NASB).

All of this may sound like lame advice if you're in the middle of a suffering situation. "Look to Jesus" comes across like a Band-Aid solution because it doesn't really take away the problem; it just gives us a different way of looking at it.

But what we *want* is relief. We want our problem or heartache to just go away. And yet the biblical message of rest is that your relief may come from the power you gain when you accept your suffering. Your relief may come from the strength you develop from serving in spite of it.

Remember that Jesus said, "Take my yoke [suffering] upon you and learn from me, for I am gentle and humble in heart, and you will find rest for your souls" (Matthew 11:29).

If you are bewildered, badgered, broken, or battered as you try to make your way along the freeways of life, take a rest. You'll find a quiet calm awaiting you when you accept what you cannot change and when you choose to serve people—even those who contribute to your pain.

8

MANAGING YOUR EXPECTATIONS

The Fifth Necessity

Indulge me for a moment. Let's flip on our turn signal and pull off the freeway for a while. There's a winding road up ahead I'd love to show you…and a little pink house that means more to me than I can describe.

The map of Pennsylvania is dotted with thousands of names of tiny villages and sleepy boroughs that make up its rural backbone. If you look a tad north of Pittsburgh and just a little east of New Castle, you'll find the word *Eastbrook* printed in the smallest type used by the mapmakers. If you go the speed limit, you can make it from one end of this little village to the other in about thirty seconds. It's the kind of town the TV classic *Hee Haw* salute was invented for. For most people, it's little more than a word on a sign that agrees with a dot on a map. But there is a handful of people who refer to this tiny collection of houses huddled around a bend in the road as their home.

See up ahead there? Right at the point of the bend? That's the house I mentioned. The one that stirs up a lot of special memories for me. It's the home of my grandmother. She and Granddad reared my mother and two uncles in this house. Granddad died when I was fairly young, but Grandma maintained that home as a fortress against the unpredictable elements that come with the passing Pennsylvania seasons—and the unpredictable tests that come with the passing of time.

Whenever my professional travels brought me close to western Pennsylvania, I grabbed as many opportunities as I could to drop in at the little pink house in Eastbrook. Crossing the threshold of her back door was like stepping through some curious time warp. But Grandma's house didn't strike you as a step backward in time as much as a visit to a place where time wasn't an issue.

She didn't divvy out time in appointments. Clocks were used for reminding her that something was in the oven or that she had twenty minutes before *Let's Make a Deal* came on. But clocks were never used to limit her availability to address people's needs. Time for her was a commodity that she invested in her family and friends.

I wish I could have bottled that special blend of scents that would meet me as I entered her house. It was a mixture of old with new, fresh with seasoned, and past with future. But as far I was concerned, in the middle of the hurried schedules that make up my typical day, it was the sweetest air in town.

Grandma was satisfied. She never struck me as a lady who felt she had been shortchanged in life. She had lived with both pain and tragedy and didn't begrudge God for either. Because she lived so much of her life for people, she had learned the joy of contentment.

The ravages of age eventually took away Grandma's eyesight. It was one personal blow that was hard to accept. But once she did, she simply resumed her role as an investor in people.

I was in the area shortly after she was moved to a full-care facility. Her house had been sold to friends, who remodeled and repainted it. (I can't believe they painted over the pink.) During the renovation, the workers accumulated a pile of lumber and trash outside. I stopped by to see the changes they were making and noticed an interesting reminder of my grandma's life on the pile next to the house.

The item that caught my eye was the instruction booklet that had come with her old wringer washing machine. It had probably sat on the back of a closet shelf for the past fifty years. I don't remember when she graduated from the wringer machine to an automatic. It was sometime after I had left childhood behind. But I do recall, while enjoying my carefree years as a child, watching Grandma set up her washing machine on laundry day.

The cycles of a wringer machine weren't regulated by an automatic internal timer but by how fast your hands could work. The clothes went from soapy water to rinse water to a dry tank through the barely parted cylinders that made up the wringer. Across the top of the wringer was a panic bar. If this type of machine served you on laundry day over a long enough period of time, you usually got an opportunity to see if the panic bar worked.

I remember one sad day when Grandma got her fingers too close to the wringers. Before she knew what had happened, the two hungry rollers had pulled her arm in up to the elbow. In the shock and pain of the moment, she didn't think to hit the panic bar. Instead, she reversed the gears and rolled her mangled arm out the way that it had gone in.

The consumption-oriented society you and I live in takes us through a wringer of a different sort. It does this in a subtle but deliberate way: it simply keeps us *unsatisfied*. Our own artificially created expectations wring rest from our hearts. They squeeze out our joy and leave our spirits dry and brittle.

No matter what we have, it isn't enough.

Regardless of the quality, it could always be better.

They don't make enlarged "We're Number Three" sponge hands to hold up at football games. We find ourselves so driven to have the best and be the best that it becomes difficult to relax and appreciate where we are and what we have along the way.

"I Can't Get No Satisfaction"

Keeping the average family unsatisfied is vital to our economic system. In order to lure me to a particular product, an advertiser must create a dissatisfaction with what I have—or a nagging desire for things I don't need.

Every time I take a shower, I stare at a good example of the persuasive power of advertising. My home came equipped with a standard shower-head fixture. It always managed to get me completely wet and adequately clean. But I kept seeing an ad on TV showing people standing under a special shower head that spun the water around and sent it pulsating over their backs. The people on the commercial were always smiling and laughing. I thought about the standard fixture on my shower. It didn't make me smile or laugh. It didn't make my scalp tingle or relax my neck. It just managed to get me completely wet and adequately clean. I *had to have* one of those shower heads that made taking a bath a holiday.

The new shower fixture cost me about five times more than the one I took off. But my back is worth it, right? I installed this new necessity for happiness about a decade ago. The last time I turned the dial from "normal" to "pulsating" was about nine years, eleven months, and three weeks ago. Mainly it has served me as a humble shower. But it does a great job of getting me completely wet and adequately clean.

Truthfully, I'm grateful to live in a free-market economy. It's a system that offers the greatest opportunities for developing ideas, accommodating needs, and enjoying prosperity. But every good thing has a potential downside. The "new and improved" nature of the most recent product makes me disappointed in the version I got just last year. If the best way to keep me coming back for more is to keep me unsatisfied, I'm going to fight an ongoing problem with restlessness. And so is my family.

I get a kick out of watching parents take their kids through the checkout lines at grocery stores. If it isn't bad enough that they bought more items than they intended to, they are forced to push their children through a narrow stall that has a couple million items they don't need within arm's length of a two-year-old. I couldn't figure out why stores created those checkout nightmares until I began noticing how many people actually succumb to the pressure to add to their four-foot-long grocery tab. Those racks filled with hundreds of toys, trinkets, and candy give even the best parents a literal run for their money. ("Yea, though I pass through the valley of the shadow of impulse, I will fear no temper tantrums because I left my kids at home.")

What I'm addressing is the very essence of restlessness. When we lose control of our expectations, we are guaranteed to be robbed of rest. Yet the culture in which we live makes losing control a foregone conclusion! If I have any hope of enjoying the rest God intends for me, I have to remind myself that I am in a constant struggle with my environment to maintain a sense of satisfaction.

When people fail to discipline their desires, they feel incomplete. A gloomy cloud of inadequacy follows them around. It's difficult to maintain deep relationships with such people—their feelings of inadequacy drain your emotions.

When people fail to discipline their desires, they place unbearable demands on a marriage. Their partner is quick to realize his or her dissatisfaction, and if the partner can't supply all that the undisciplined spouse wants, the partner feels a sense of failure.

When people fail to discipline their desires, they compound stress in their children. An environment where the best is always in the future breeds an attitude that makes the present look cheap.

When people fail to discipline their desires, they accommodate the powers within the world system that desire to control them. A heart that finds it hard to accept its position in life is putty in the hands of the powers of darkness.

When God etched the Ten Commandments into the stones Moses had brought up on the mountain, He used the first and last commandments as the supports for the other eight. They were sweeping statements that served as catchalls for the wandering passions of humans. If we view these as guidelines for contentment (which they are), we'll see why it makes such logical sense to place them in the order in which they appear in the Bible.

The first commandment says:

> I am the LORD your God, who brought you out of the land
> of Egypt, out of the house of slavery. You shall have no other
> gods before Me. (Exodus 20:2–3, NASB)

A focused affection on the God who sets people free is the best way to enjoy a life of balanced love. God is love. He is the essence of its definition. Since love is one of the fundamental needs of humans, it stands to reason that we need to begin by loving the Author of love. As we maintain and strengthen our love for Him, we enable our hearts to see the second priority of our existence on earth—people—in proper perspective.

The last commandment says:

> You shall not covet your neighbor's house; you shall not covet
> your neighbor's wife or his male servant or his female servant
> or his ox or his donkey or anything that belongs to your
> neighbor. (v. 17)

Coveting has a lot of nasty synonyms—envy, jealousy, lust, greed. It starts in our hearts as a seed but gets watered and fertilized by the inevitable pressures on our pride.

Your best friend gets a promotion with a significant pay raise, and the seed germinates. The new models for next year roll into the showroom at the car dealerships, and the seed sprouts roots.

You go shopping with your best friend, and she fits beautifully into dresses that are the same size she wore when she got married fifteen years ago. You stare at the size inside the dress you're holding and notice that it's gone up four digits since your wedding day. Ah, the seed of coveting is now starting to sprout above the surface of your personality.

Coveting is material inebriation. It's a craving for things that don't last and an addiction to things that don't really matter. It forces us to depend on tomorrow to bring us the happiness that today couldn't supply.

Contentment Is an Attitude

One autumn several years ago, I was flying to Canada to speak at a college. I was on a British carrier with many Europeans on board. The reservations computer had seated me next to a husband and wife in their midfifties. They were a Jewish couple from England who had been vacationing in the United States. Other than smiling and saying hello as I sat down, I didn't say anything to them for the first hour and a half of our flight. Instead I enjoyed being privy to a fascinating conversation between a husband and wife who had been through a lot together. Trust me, it wasn't eavesdropping. They were so entirely caught up in their conversation about family, business, music, fine wines, and politics that it was impossible to shut them out. I didn't want to anyway. These were the kind of people you'd choose for companions if you had to be stuck in a lifeboat for a couple weeks.

Midway through dinner, the British couple invited me into their conversation by utilizing the normal small-talk questions. My questions to them were a lot more probing. (Minding other people's business is part of my job.) I learned about their business endeavors in England, of their wayward son, of their personal yearning to die in Israel, and of how their ability to dream at all was nearly dashed as children. Both narrowly escaped Hitler's gas chambers. She lost her parents at Dachau. He wasn't sure how his parents perished.

I asked them what I thought was an intelligent question.

"Are you happy?"

Neither of them spoke for a second. Then this wise Jewish gentleman made a smirking sound and slowly shook his head as he stared straight in front of him.

"You Americans. The bottom line with you is, 'Are you happy?' You want to make sure that when all is said and done, you *feel* a certain way. That requires life to be fair, generous, and free from hassles. Life has been very unfair to us. We have made, lost, and made again a fortune of this world's goods. We've never really known a time when we didn't have to battle fear and uncertainty. But we never approached life as if it owed us something. We have had the opportunity to love and to hope. What more could we need?"

Wise reprimands should be viewed as gifts. I realized that this decent man had taken the time and risk to be honest. In the process he gave me a gift that I could enjoy for a lifetime.

It is so easy to fall into the trap of "needing" something emotional or superficial before you'll allow yourself to find contentment. But I learned (from two people who should know) that contentment doesn't require a formula; it requires an attitude. They had a gentle and quiet peace in their hearts that I envied. They weren't living life for what they could get but for what they had. And because they didn't demand anything from life, life had a hard time letting them down. They were serious and disciplined stewards of their expectations.

They did not covet what they did not possess.

"Greener Grass" Syndrome

I'm amazed how often people end up envying the very people who envy them! A pastor sat back in his chair, listening to the man seated across from him complain about the cross God had given him to bear. This prominent parishioner was regretting that he had chosen the line of work he was in. He knew he should be grateful. After all, since he'd bought the majority position in the company, the stock had split twice. The P. and L. statements for the last three years had supplied him with excellent Christmas bonuses. He and his wife had enjoyed visits to Europe, Asia, Australia, and most recently, the former Soviet Union.

But this man fought a lot of guilt.

He had once pursued the pulpit, but took a side road in seminary that placed him in the marketplace for good. He went on to outline how much he envied the pastor's knowledge of the Bible and his grasp of theology. He wished that *he* had time to sit around and read the Scriptures all day. Furthermore...

The pastor looked past the man's tailored slacks and gold watch to the window through which he could see the two cars parked outside his study. They were the same color, but that was as far as the similarities went. As soon as this appointment was over, he would drive his aging Pontiac home so his wife could borrow it to do her errands. The odometer broke at seventy-eight thousand miles three years ago. As his counselee rambled on about what a spiritual loser he was, the pastor studied the picture framed on the corner of his desk. His two children smiled so broadly and so proudly. They were too young to be self-conscious. But in a few years they'd realize what he already knew: their teeth needed elaborate orthodontic work. But it wasn't going to happen on his paycheck. And deep down inside, he resented it. He kept thinking of all the times businessmen had said to him, "Pastor, with your skills, you could have knocked 'em dead in the business arena."

Changing places wouldn't solve either one of these men's problems. One man was an ungrateful steward of much; the other was an ungrateful steward of many.

The more we measure our significance by other people's accomplishments and acquisitions, the less we'll be able to feel at rest in our daily lives. Comparison is a poison pill. A rushed and anxious lifestyle is only going to bring more successful people to envy, more unaffordable conveniences to covet, and more failures to regret.

Attitudes That Hinder

Certain attitudes predispose a person to envy. Envy is guaranteed to bring unhappiness. But because no man is an island, an unsatisfied attitude will also take its toll on people close to you. A marriage can find itself paralyzed by discontent. A wife might be discontented with the take-home amount on her husband's paycheck, and a husband might be discontented with the size of his wife's chest. It's a flawed kind of love that consistently makes the other person feel like he or she doesn't measure up. And our children can pick up this same attitude early enough to punish us with ungrateful spirits throughout their stay under our influence.

Here's the good news. We can teach ourselves to be satisfied just as certainly as we can teach ourselves to be unsatisfied. If certain attitudes predispose us to envy, then we need to run an inventory of those attitudes and move them toward satisfaction. It's a way to monitor our hearts and to force them back on target.

One way to check your satisfaction quota is to see how you complete four sentences. The second half of these statements can tell all. Let me help by completing them several ways. I may not hit the areas you struggle with, but the ones I do offer should give you an idea of how to personalize them:

If only I had…
> a job
> a better job
> a more understanding boss
> enough money to retire
> a bigger house
> a thinner waist
> a better education
> a husband
> a different husband

a child
a lifestyle like...
a more respectful family

If only I hadn't...
dropped out of school
been forced to get married
had an abortion
started drinking
struck that child with my car
been fired
run up so many debts
trusted that smooth-talking con artist
neglected my wife
quit that job
sold that stock
bought that stock

If only they had...
given me more playing time
recognized my potential
offered me that position
encouraged me to apply myself in school
supported me in my efforts
been honest with me
stuck with me

If only they hadn't...
abandoned me as a baby
discouraged me
prejudged me
pushed me so hard to achieve

lied to me
been so interested in making money
been ashamed of my handicap

If only… The starting words for unfulfilled expectations or nagging regrets. No one is immune to their destructive impact. Because we're people and not machines, we can't deny the impact of our past mistakes or disappointments. Nor can we turn deaf ears or blind eyes to the many desires of this world that may be out of reach.

Dealing with a Disappointing Past

Too many people are unsatisfied with where they are in life because they don't like the path they took to get there. Often the path to the present was not of their personal choosing.

Most people have had to deal with the pain that comes when they don't meet other people's expectations. But all rejection is not created equal. The pain of being rejected by a parent or spouse is far more devastating than being rejected for our ideas or unappreciated for our contributions by some minion at work. Some people can't seem to move out of neutral in the present because their primary "reason for living" let them down in the past.

Others get their life in gear but take off in the wrong direction. A disappointing past can throw our expectations out of whack. We suddenly view acquisitions or status as an antidote to the pain we've had to endure in the past. We think success will prove that we can amount to something, marriage will prove that we are worth loving, wealth will get people's attention.

I remember an enlightening conversation I had with a plastic surgeon. Much of his work brought a healthy transformation to his patients. A rebuilt nose could bring an end to years of teasing. A restructured jaw could restore what the disfigurement of an accident had stolen. "But you know, Tim," he confided, "many people come into my office for a new look when what they really want is a new *life*."

A key, then, to experiencing lasting rest in our lives is refusing to merely rely on superficial solutions to past disappointments. We need to keep our past hurts in perspective.

Thankfully we don't have to do this alone. The message of the Bible is that God wants to comfort us in our sorrows, fill our voids, and forgive our sins. There is no earthly purchase that will remove the pain of rejection. There is no project or activity that will cover the consequences of our negligence. In our emptiness and pain, we need the permanent presence of a God who promises never to leave us or let us down. When our past is handled in a healthy way, we have a much better chance of having healthy expectations.

Is It Okay to Dream?

Of course, there's a healthy desire within most of us to improve ourselves and our positions. This is an instinctive quality placed within us by God. To deny it would be foolish, and to ignore it would be sacrilegious.

Certain additions to our lives are capable of bringing a lot of joy. A bigger house could offer some badly needed relief from the cramped quarters you presently endure. A graduate degree could offer you a better platform from which to serve people and a better income through which you could accommodate your family's needs. An exotic vacation could allow you to make many beautiful memories with people you love. A spouse could give you an opportunity to love and be loved. There's nothing wrong with having these desires.

But if you're going to dream, you need to make sure you're doing two things at the same time.

First, you need to make sure that *you are pursuing legitimate goals.* What is a legitimate goal? Anything that improves your ability to love God and serve people. Is there room, then, for acquiring things that primarily accommodate you? Sure. Beautiful possessions and nice creature comforts have a legitimate place in a balanced person's life. Possessions can never "complete" you, but they can be rewards that come from hard work and conscientious living. They may adorn a life, but they don't *make* a life. To pursue possessions in order to fill a void is folly. And if in the process of pursuing them you neglect your God-given responsibilities, then they are double trouble. Instead of being rewards, they become treacherous obstacles to healthy living.

If you could've joined me on a visit to a particular woman I'm thinking about, you would know exactly what I mean. I met Marilyn and her family the way a lot of family advocates meet people for the first time—through their pain. She and her husband had nearly lost their son through a terrible accident. The boy had been thrown from his dirt bike while racing through the desert. It only took a split second for the little boy's body to be mangled and a family's heart to be broken. Most families would have come apart under the weight and pain this accident brought, but Marilyn's resolve and God's grace made the difference. She refused to accept defeat. She prayed that boy out of a coma, out of bed, out of a wheelchair, and finally out of crutches. It was a tribute to her love and persistence.

Several years after the accident, I stopped by Marilyn's home to visit her and her son. I drove up to a nice house in a great community. The inside of the home was even better. It was comfortably furnished, tastefully decorated, and extremely roomy. After chatting in the family room for a while, we all moved into the kitchen so she could get us a soft drink. I couldn't help noticing her refrigerator door. Instead of the typical family collage, it was covered with pictures of mansions, sleek yachts, exotic places, and actual piles of cash. Naturally I inquired about them. She was happy to tell me all about it.

After her son had recovered from the worst of his injuries, she and her husband decided to make a career move. Their new employers dangled promises of riches beyond the average person's imagination. They were working day and night to build their profile in the company. They regularly attended sales meetings, where articulate company leaders made them feel inadequate. They were reminded that where they were was inferior to where they could be. They were told to dream without limits, to visualize themselves enjoying the very best life could offer. Their boss encouraged them to put pictures on their refrigerator and bathroom mirror of the things they thought would bring them a lot of joy. They were told not to accept "mediocrity and second best" but to go for the top.

I looked around her house. It seemed so warm and comfortable. Definitely upper middle class.

Then I looked at the boy.

I thought of Jesus raising Jairus's daughter from the dead. Although He hadn't worked in an instantaneous way with this woman's son, his recovery was no less a miracle. Her boy was supposed to be dead, but he was very much alive. Doctors had said that if he did live, he'd be a vegetable. Instead he was mentally alert. They said that if he did come out of the coma, he'd probably never walk again. But he proved them wrong once more by starring on his school's track team.

His mother walked me to my car. When the boy was out of earshot, I voiced my concern about the shift in her preoccupations. She had been given a healthy chunk of earth's material pleasures, but even more importantly she had her son back from the dead. Why was she so obsessed with getting more? She tried to defend herself. Wealth, she said, would give her a greater "platform" from which to tell the story of her son. Wealth would help her influence people for Christ. The resources could be used to finance the message.

I closed the car door and rolled down the window. I wanted to be honest with her, but the words came slow and hard.

"Marilyn…you're trying so hard to rationalize wrong priorities. If the only way you can gain an audience's respect is by outshining them materially, you're doomed to have fickle friends all your life."

If the only way to get someone to listen to her was to shout from the deck of her yacht or over the whine of her private jet, she was in trouble. The truth was that she wasn't satisfied with what she had—and never would be.

She and her husband pursued the wrong dreams. Ultimately their marriage blew apart, and their second child ended up in court on drug charges. They pursued legitimate things for illegitimate reasons. Instead of letting them become rewards of conscientious work, they became obsessions of an unsatisfied and restless heart.

Don't be snookered by what you see on *MTV Cribs* or on reruns of *Lifestyles of the Rich and Famous*. Material acquisition cannot fill the void within our lives. Status and influence cannot substitute for our need to love and be loved. You want proof? Trace the trail of broken marriages and troubled children that plague many of the people showcased on those television shows.

No, there is nothing wrong with living comfortably, dressing well, driving a nice car, or being famous. These are legitimate rewards that always have responsibilities attached to them. But when they become the things that drive us, complete us, or sustain us, we're sure to wake up one morning and find ourselves empty. Hollow to the core.

Billy Graham put it well when he said that the smallest package he ever saw was a man wrapped up wholly in himself. Undisciplined desires can make small packages out of big people. Jesus said, "Seek first His kingdom and His righteousness, and all these things [the necessities that sustain and satisfy] will be added to you" (Matthew 6:33, NASB).

Bringing Contentment on Board

Remember how I said we need to be doing two things in order to maintain disciplined desires? The first thing is to make sure we're pursuing legitimate goals. The second thing is to *make sure that we are making the most of where we are*. You know what I mean. You've seen people who are so busy stretching for the brass ring that they forget to enjoy the ride on the merry-go-round.

We need to make Contentment a member of our internal board of directors. Give him the freedom to ask the hard questions when you start feeling that you need something more to bring you happiness. If you do, be prepared to mumble a lot to yourself. He likes to ask questions such as:

- Can you afford this?
- Do you have to give up the few spare hours you have left to take advantage of this thing?
- Will this free you up to spend the time necessary to maintain your commitments to family and friends?
- Will this in any way frustrate your relationship with God?

Do you see why people don't want Contentment in the boardroom of their hearts? He demands that we place proper value on the superficial things we believe will bring us greater happiness.

An unsatisfied heart in a life filled with blessings is sin. As long as we allow this constant craving to dominate our hearts, we will be denied inner rest. As Calvin Miller wrote, "The world is poor because her fortune is buried in the sky and all her treasure maps are of the earth."[10]

The only way we can keep our expectations and desires disciplined is with God's help. A relationship with God that is personal yields a set of desires that is practical. Knowing that He loves us and has forgiven us keeps us from wanting the wrong things. By following His example when He walked the earth, we can develop priorities that will sustain our heart both now and through the future.

9

MANAGING YOUR STRENGTHS

The Sixth Necessity

uthor John Trent tells of an eye-opening incident on his first day in graduate school. He had enrolled at Dallas Theological Seminary with good intentions, but since arriving he seriously wondered if he would make it. He walked into his first class with legitimate apprehensions. After all, this wasn't "party time" college anymore. This was an environment where fifty-dollar theological words rolled off professors' tongues. The dean had made it clear in orientation that Dallas wouldn't spoon-feed anyone. Either you kept up with the workload or you would find yourself in an unrecoverable position.

The assistant had just passed out the syllabus for the class, and after reading it John mentally calculated that he was already three weeks behind. The professor stepped up to the lectern and stared around the room at the sea of faces. John felt like he could read the man's mind: *"So this is the leadership of tomorrow's church? We're in trouble!"* Despite this unnerving scrutiny, everything John had heard about this man underscored that he was a loving and caring gentleman. Dr. Howard Hendricks was one of the main reasons he had enrolled at Dallas.

The very first words out of the professor's mouth sent ice water through John's veins: "Gentlemen, I am going to give you the most significant test you will ever have during your studies here at Dallas Seminary."

John groaned silently. *So much for all the nice things I heard about this guy.*

"How you do on this test will determine how you do in the ministry."

Great, I'm getting cut from the team before I even get a chance to play.

"Those who do well invariably succeed. Those who flunk this test will invariably struggle and falter in ministry."

You're not wasting any time separating the sheep from the goats, are you, Prof? I knew I should've had more theological training before I came here. He's going to split some theological hair and make me look like an idiot.

"On the three-by-five card in front of you, I want you to list your three greatest weaknesses."

That's it? That's all? What I'm lousy at? Piece of cake! If being a success just takes a working knowledge of my inadequacies, then I'm gonna be one of the greatest Christian workers the church has ever had.

John joined his fellow seminarians in writing down their weaknesses. They all wrote quickly. The only problem any of them seemed to have was deciding *which* of their many weaknesses would be considered the top three. John finished writing, laid down his pen, and stared up at the professor with a look of confidence on his face.

Dr. Hendricks continued. "Now, folks, turn over your card and answer this second question."

I knew it was too good to be true! Here comes the zinger. I'm doomed. Maybe it's not too late to get back some of my tuition...

"What are your three greatest *strengths?*"

John joined his colleagues in experiencing temporary paralysis in his writing hand. This time students weren't rushing to fill out their card. Some simply stared at it. Others tapped the tip of their nose with their pen or frowned intently at the wall as though they hoped to find the answer written on it.

Answering that question seemed, well, contradictory to John's calling. He was supposed to be a humble man of the cloth. Listing his greatest strengths seemed like cheap boasting. Wasn't there something in the Bible about God giving grace to the humble and opposing the proud? Zeroing in on what made him strong—and even superior—to his fellow human beings, was discomfiting. Besides, God gets a lot of mileage out of working through people's weaknesses. Didn't He say to Paul, "My grace is sufficient for you, for [my] power is perfected in weakness" (2 Corinthians 12:9, NASB)?

A few desk rows over and a few seats back from John, another young man sat struggling with the same question—and these many decades later, I still struggle with it.

Dr. Hendricks was right. Knowledge of our personal strengths is critical to a calm and ordered life. It's easy enough to list our weaknesses—all of us have had plenty of help on that score. Parents, teachers, coaches, friends, and enemies have made sure we don't overlook a single one.

It has been my observation that most people grow up with lots of negative reinforcement. Our culture occasionally rewards but seldom remembers those who come in second. The list of those who "also ran" doesn't get much space in the yearbook. The last time I checked, "close" only counts in horseshoes and nuclear war.

It's easy to focus on our failures and weaknesses. And if asked to, most of us are ready to conduct a guided tour through our inadequacies at a moment's notice. But the fact remains that you and I *do* have strengths, God-given resources worth developing and managing. And if we want to cope with the incredible pressures of our hurried world, we need to isolate those strengths and put them to work. It's a matter of stewardship.

The word *stewardship* isn't used as much as it used to be, but it's an excellent word for our discussion. It refers among other things to the *conscientious management of the things that really matter.* It requires responsibility and maturity. Stewardship demands work and doesn't accept excuses. It forces people to reevaluate priorities and makes them reconsider their purposes for living.

When I meet older people who advise me to slow down, spend more time with others, and develop my talents, I hear the voice of experience talking. They have learned through waste and regret what God would rather teach us through principles of stewardship—that resources are to be conserved and invested, not ignored or squandered.

Although I'm not quite to the age where I can speak from the wisdom of decades upon decades of seasoned years of experience, I do have a head of gray hair and have raised four kids. Most of the unhappy people who approach me for counsel suffer from a simple syndrome: they are poor stewards of their lives. They have developed a bad habit of ignoring the important and prioritizing the nonessential.

There is only one way out of this dilemma, and few are willing to take it. The path to relief is painful. It requires reordering priorities— deliberately changing the inner price tags we attach to the components of our lives. For some people that's just too much. They would rather accept the discomfort and slow death of emotional cancer than endure the surgery that could save them.

It's too bad, because this sixth key for genuine rest could give them the platform and the discipline to maintain the other five.

When Dr. Hendricks challenged John and me to isolate and articulate our greatest strengths, he wasn't asking us to be boastful, haughty, or proud. He was calling us to be realistic, honest, and conscientious. He knew that life becomes a threat to our contentment when we consistently take from it but seldom give back. He knew that we become a drain on people if we *use* relationships rather than *contribute* to them. He knew that our greatest joy would be found in investing our gifts rather than burying them.

His kind of thinking comes from the presupposition that every man and woman is born *rich*. We may come into the world in our birthday suit and leave in our burial clothing, but our greatest treasures are wrapped up in the things that can't be kept in a safe-deposit box. We are born with intrinsic value—the very essence of God's heart.

God wouldn't sacrifice His Son for someone who has no value.

He wouldn't give eternal life to someone who has no significance.

It might help us, as we develop this discussion on managing our gifts, to divide our true assets into three categories: *calling, convictions,* and *capabilities*. These groupings can serve as a checklist as you determine what kind of steward you are.

Stewarding Our Calling

Part of the frustration of the hurried life is that it has a way of trivializing our commitments. We have certain callings in life that must be maintained, but life hassles us into giving these callings second-class status. I'm not referring to *calling* in a mystical sense. I don't know anything about that kind of stuff. But I do know there are certain responsibilities we are either given or choose to accept that cannot be ignored.

Vocational Callings

I think of my calling as a minister, for example. I may work under the wing of an independent ministry and I may speak at different churches each Sunday, but I am, nonetheless, a minister. If you were to visit my office, you would notice the framed diplomas and the ordination certificate that serve as visible credentials of my calling. I have a close friend who has debated with me at length about how I knew I was called to the ministry. Although I have done a poor job of explaining to him how I knew I was supposed to be a minister, we both agree this is what I'm supposed to be doing.

Because of my calling, I must maintain certain responsibilities. My freedoms are limited. People's expectations are high. Because of my role as teacher, helper, and advisor, my calling requires me to be a learner. I can't coast, and I can't fake it. I can't drop pearls of wisdom from a small window in an ivory tower. The people I serve deserve messages wrung from the crucible of my daily experience and walk with God. The people who look to me for direction need to know that my advice is more than theory or regurgitation of grad school textbooks. If I'm going to prepare them for daily battle, I have to smell of gunpowder and know my way around the trenches.

My calling restricts me, but it is in submission to those restrictions that I become most valuable to people. It goes with the territory of serving. There are many professions that call for serious commitments—and restrictions—from those who work within them. Doctors, teachers, managers, researchers, public servants, and attorneys all work in fields that call for a high level of commitment. We must steward our profession well. If someone has either chosen or accepted a position as a role model to young people, for example, that person has forfeited certain rights. That's why sports figures need to think twice before they exercise their independence in areas that could mislead children. Jesus said that people who lead children astray will not do so without consequences. (His language is actually a lot stronger than that. Read it for yourself in Matthew 18:6.)

When we are good stewards of our calling, we counter the pressures of a hurried lifestyle. Hurried lifestyles push us to take shortcuts. Too many of them cost us in the areas of honesty and self-esteem. When we feel that we are cheating those for whom or with whom we are called to work, something within us breaks down. We can't expect to defraud ourselves and still feel calm inside.

Relational Callings

On August 19, 1972, I stood before a group of witnesses and said that I would devote my life to Darcy Dirks. I wasn't drugged, drunk, or hallucinating when I said it. The two witnesses who signed our marriage license will testify to that. Since then there have been opportunities to go back on my word. Furthermore, my wife and I have given each other reasons to wish we hadn't been so quick to agree to the vows.

Nevertheless, the vows were exchanged. The contract was signed. It became one of my callings in life—a calling that God takes very seriously. The more seriously I take my calling as a husband, the better off my marriage.

On four occasions my wife went to the hospital to give birth to children who exhibit a lot of my physical characteristics. The moment they were conceived, they became part of my calling. As a steward of my calling to fatherhood, I cannot hope to come close to meeting their needs without a deliberate and individual devotion to each one of them.

This is when our high-speed world really puts on the pressure. Being an effective father and being a "success" in the workplace at the same time is sometimes impossible. When it comes to choices in this area, the lure of the fast lane increases its pull. Kids don't cooperate as well as the laws of money. Kids don't reward our egos as much as the shiny steps at the top of the ladder of success. That's why the sixth key to rest carries so much clout. It's the acid test of our priorities. If we are good stewards of our callings, we will consistently refuse to sacrifice the permanent on the altar of the immediate. We will place our callings in divine order. Regardless of how noble our vocation and how many people directly benefit from our involvement in it, God will not condone the forsaking of our primary callings (marriage and children) for a secondary calling (like a vocation).

Stewarding Our Convictions

Some people paint themselves into a restless corner by failing to maintain their convictions. We've already considered in an earlier chapter the sad outcome of those who refuse to live within the limits.

Convictions represent an incredible source of strength to the individual who embraces them with unwavering consistency. Maybe you've never seen them in that light before. Maybe you've never included them in an inventory of your personal resources. And yet your personal convictions must be counted among your most precious possessions. The pressures to conform, to ignore, to excuse, or to surrender bombard us every day. If I want to maintain a calm heart in the midst of a hectic culture, I must be careful not to compromise my convictions.

Convictions are an asset to our spirit and a resource for our relationships. They function as the cement within our love, the strength within our purpose, and the resolve within our hope. And they must be guarded with a passion. Without consistent convictions, an individual finds himself at the mercy of life's shifting winds. (A good passage of Scripture on this subject is James 1:6–8.)

Too many people think that ethics can be determined by situational circumstances. Yet making the rules more convenient as you go along is certain to produce conflict both inside and outside your heart. Feelings get hurt. Lives get damaged beyond repair. That's why we can't afford to ignore the impact of convictions.

Please note, however, that convictions have nothing to do with the collective conscience of our society. The collective conscience is no more qualified to determine truth than the individual. Sometimes the collective conscience is little more than the pooling of mass ignorance. If the majority is to be our standard, we're in serious trouble. The will of the majority should never be allowed to trump the will of God. If we want to steward convictions, we must always let God have the first word...and the last.

That's why a steady diet of Bible reading and study is so crucial to the well-managed life. The Word's pages contain universal truths we can rely on when we aren't sure of what to do. In my work, I run into all kinds of people. Those who make it through life with the least number of conflicts from their personal choices are those who submit to a clear set of convictions. And those who submit to convictions invariably maintain a consistent intake of God's Word. I'm not legalistic about when or how often a person must read the Scriptures. I just know that those who go to the Bible on a habitual basis to gain direction for living consistently make better choices than those who minimize their exposure to God's Word.

When our convictions are worth fighting for, we become an invaluable asset to our culture. People who are willing to lay their popularity and status on the line for the underdogs, victims, and legitimate causes of life ensure that there will be a tomorrow worth fighting for.

In a restless world where rules are relative and people vacillate from one urgency to the next, convictions will set you free. They will support you when you are alone, defend you when you are attacked, and exonerate you when you are falsely accused. They may be the only friend you have at certain dark moments of your life. But if you steward them well, they can give you a solid reputation, a secure marriage, confident kids, a stable career, and maybe even save your life.

Those who love the truth will live by it. Those who live by it will enjoy a complete and balanced life. The Bible promises peace and rest to the individual who stewards his convictions. Psalms 1 and 15 are excellent studies in the power of consistent convictions. As David summarizes in Psalm 15:5, "He who does these things will never be shaken."

Maintaining our callings and managing our convictions will enable us to steward the third major treasure of our lives.

Stewarding Our Capabilities

Every person has talent. When talents are harnessed and disciplined, they become skills. When skills are used, power is unleashed. And when power is used to contribute to a legitimate purpose, people benefit. Individuals who steward their personal capabilities make their lives part of the cultural solution to frustration and confusion.

But too many people run into problems because stewarding our capabilities is hard. It means denying oneself, sacrificing, and yes, even failing in order to perfect our giftings. From early childhood, we can pick up the patterns that either reward us for our efforts or punish us for our negligence. The one pattern that seems to dominate the lives of teenagers I work with is their struggle to delay gratification. It might be in the area of studies, sports, a job, or sex—regardless, the outcome is the same. When teens are unable to discipline themselves and channel their talents and skills in proper directions, they experience an inner restlessness that shows. They are angry, frustrated, doomed to suffer through life until they become willing to submit their strengths to personal discipline.

Well-managed talents, on the other hand, give a person a strong sense of purpose and value. They help us to counter the overwhelming pressures from culture that make us feel insecure. Insecure people are never static with their insecurity. Invariably they impose their insecurities on the people around them. Most insecurities are difficult to overlook; they are deep-seated and complex. But one remedy is to develop the ability to harness your capabilities and use them in a positive way.

Every Christian has spiritual gifts. These were given by God in order to make the church well rounded. Attending church Sunday after Sunday without serving is poor stewardship of our capabilities. I've always found it ironic that the people who seem to demand the most help from the church for their personal problems are consistently the ones who serve the least. It's too bad because God can bring us a depth of joy and stability when we are carefully guarding and using the talents and gifts He has given us for His glory.

Of course, every dimension of our lives requires balance and boundaries. Talents are our personal strengths. But poorly maintained talents can become overtaxed. In many people's lives, their weaknesses are nothing more than strengths pushed to the limit. If we push our spiritual gifts to an extreme, we burn out. If we push our emotional gifts to an extreme, we get depressed. If we push our physical and intellectual gifts to an extreme, we get sick.

Probably the biggest battle most of us fight is with the stewarding of our time. It's the one gift in our life that was given to us in a fixed amount. Each time we use it, it is forever spent. That's why we should be careful to invest generous chunks of it in things and people that have eternal significance. Don't fall into the trap of thinking that only those who wear the cleric's collar or nun's habit have the opportunity to invest in forever. The little eyes that peek at you through the rails of a crib or the spouse who sleeps inches from you every night can make your gift of time an investment in eternity.

When Stewardship Comes Home

I mentioned earlier in the book that my mother died of cancer. From the time the doctors discovered it to the time it took her life was only five months. Her decline was swift and unstoppable. Surgery, radiation, and chemotherapy had no effect.

Mom had been a serious steward of the things that mattered. She never forsook her calling as a wife and mother. She didn't require an opinion poll to determine which way she should lean in a conflict. Her convictions served her just fine. And she isolated her talents as a servant early in her married life. She gave to her family and friends from a generous heart.

A few weeks before her allotted gift of time was up, she was hanging on to this life by an invisible thread and the many visible tubes and equipment around her bed. The intensive care unit of the old hospital in Greenville, Pennsylvania, is a circular room. The beds surround a central hub where the nurses monitor the vital signs that come from the various patients' equipment. The only thing that gives privacy to a patient is a curtain that can be pulled around the bed. There is one exception though—a single room built into the circle for extremely ill patients.

That's where Mom lay dying.

My younger brother and I had flown back to see her three times in the five months she was sick. During the last month, I called every morning to see how she made it through the night and every night to see how she made it through the day. My father stayed by her side. My three other brothers and my sister all lived in the area. They stopped by regularly, almost daily, to be with her.

Shortly before Mom died, a wealthy and influential member of that small Pennsylvania community was admitted to the intensive care unit for observation. On the third night of his stay in the hospital, he had a discussion with the nurse who was preparing him to go to sleep for the night. I called the unit shortly after she finished working with him. She couldn't help but relate their conversation.

This young nurse was a Christian. She knew of our family's love for Christ and of my mother's quiet but compelling testimony. She told me that the man she had talked with was one of the most powerful men in the community. He wielded great influence, even at the hospital. Yet he had languished in that hospital room for three days without a single visitor. He had a wife and children, but they had not come by.

As she was giving him his medicine, he inquired about the patient in the private room.

"Oh, that's Mrs. Kimmel," the nurse replied.

He wanted to know about my father and my brothers and sister. She told him all about them and mentioned that Mrs. Kimmel's two sons in Phoenix had been back to see her several times and called daily to check on her status.

He asked about Mom's condition.

"Mrs. Kimmel will die any day," the nurse told him. "If she lives a week, we'll all be surprised."

At that point this man of influence dropped his head back on his pillow and got quiet. Just before the nurse walked away, he looked up at her with tears in his eyes. "You know?" he said in a husky voice. "I would gladly trade places with Mrs. Kimmel and die a week from now, if for that week, I could have a family who cared enough about me not to make me die alone."

The words of Eleanor Roosevelt ring true:

> One's philosophy is not best expressed in words. It is
> expressed in the choices one makes. In the long run, we
> shape our lives and we shape ourselves. The process never
> ends until we die. And the choices we make are ultimately
> our responsibility.[11]

PART

3

LITTLE HOUSE
ON THE INTERNET

When his cell phone rang the first time, no one at the birthday party gave it a second thought. That's what cell phones do. But when he followed that incoming call with four outgoing ones (one that lasted almost fifteen minutes), took one more incoming call, and also sent out two e-mails, people started wondering why he'd even bothered to come to the party. And if that wasn't enough, he downloaded a podcast of *Sports Central* to check out the status of his office bracket for March Madness.

Actually, there was a good reason why he should be at the party... an extremely good reason. His three-year-old son was the guest of honor. The house was crowded with a dozen kids and their respective parents, all of whom had come to celebrate this wonderful milestone in a little boy's life. They had slipped away from their busy schedules and demanding responsibilities long enough to show a young man how significant he was and how glad they were that he had been born—all except one of them. The one person who had contributed a large portion of the birthday boy's DNA was what you might call "present but unaccounted for." His son waited quietly but anxiously, along with all the other guests, as the candles on the cake burned their way closer and closer to the icing. Finally his dad finished the last conversation on his cell phone and came in from the patio so everyone could sing the boy his special song and applaud as he blew out his candles.

It's hard to say what the little boy wished for as he extinguished those three waning flames, but most of the adults at the party were wishing that his father would disconnect from all the technology that tethered him to the outside world long enough to notice his son.

The Call of the Wireless

If you haven't been to a gathering like this, just wait—you'll eventually end up at one. Such occurrences have become far more common as we've grown more and more accustomed to living our lives in the passing lane of the information superhighway. The miniaturizing of microchip memory has made it easy and inexpensive for us to carry an outlet to millions upon millions of demanding forces in a tiny device that fits easily into our pockets. And only a few people in the Western world would dare leave home without one.

We've become a generation of restless people operating at the beck and call of a digital world. We're wired on wireless. But it is barbed wireless if we don't know what we're doing. Left unchecked, this obsession can snag our hearts and entangle itself around our spirits until it completely controls us. Bondage to technology has a bad habit of estranging us from the human drama constantly playing out around us.

I've watched many dads miss once-in-a-lifetime opportunities with their kids so they can stay on top of some business deal when their higher calling as fathers assumed that they should be creating foundational memories for the next generation. I've observed nice moms, loving moms, who let technology become the tail wagging the dog in their vital role of transferring meaning and purpose to their children's lives.

Here's reality: Raising kids for true greatness requires a carefully connected relationship with the *heart* of a child. Grooming kids for a confident run at adulthood requires a lot of face time when they're young. It requires more lap time than laptop time, more links to emotions than to e-mails. Without even trying, any family can find itself little more than a collection of human silos living under the same roof while holed up in their own private cyberworlds.

If we don't have a carefully thought-out strategy, the hurried world of technology can steal our joy and undermine our priorities to our spouse, our kids, our friends, and God. Chat rooms can provide a place to hide from the responsibility married people have to stay closely connected to the heart of a spouse and to meet his or her sexual needs.

The endless corridors of online shopping on the World Wide Web can hold us in a transfixed stupor for hours each day at the expense of actually living an engaging life with our friends. The most benign sounds coming from our computer, cell phone, or PDA often get to enjoy siren status for too many people. The slightest bleep from one of these devices can stop people midsentence and pull them away from a significant conversation with someone they love in order to give their undivided attention to a wrong number. And it still baffles me how often I hear people say that they can't find a window to spend any quiet and reflective moments with God each day, but they can always find time to check and respond to their e-mail.

Separating the Sheep from the Goats... Technically Speaking

The birthday party we peeked in on at the beginning of this chapter lends itself to a quick overview of the way many people deal with their online lives.

There's the misguided father of the birthday boy. Obviously this man is making a series of bad choices. But if you pinned him down, he'd most likely have a well-entrenched defense for why it's impossible to actually step away from any of the technological devices that connect him to the outside world—even for the hour or two it takes to stop and celebrate his son's big day.

Our Internet world has duped millions of people into a superficial state of their own self-importance. I've talked to fathers like this one over the years, and invariably they defer to the importance of whatever deal they have in motion at the time. Their work is omnipotent. The success of the deal is contingent on one immediate response after another. Often they mention the large sums of money that are at risk and the powerful people on the other end of the wireless line. These are forces that don't take kindly to being subordinated—even for the few moments it takes to hold a cake in front of your three-year-old son, sing "Happy Birthday," and cheer as he blows out his candles.

I've even heard guys defend their reasons for maintaining an almost seamless line of statistics regarding their basketball bracket during the month of March with the excuse, "I've got a lot of money on the line." One guy I know actually used his cell phone during worship at church to check the final scores of games he knew were ending about that time! Even though he had absolutely no control over the actual wins and losses of the teams involved, he still felt it necessary to interrupt his focused attention on God in order to check up on the scores—scores that would be *exactly the same* had he waited until he was home.

It's fairly obvious to anyone with even a minimal understanding of relationships that when technology has this kind of a throat-hold on an individual, it's just a matter of time before all the meaningful relationships in his or her life quietly erode into a neutral state of apathy. Yet too many people continue to allow the high-tech world to lead them around by the nose. The good news is that all the money these people have made at the expense of paying attention to their roles as parents will come in handy when the therapist's bill arrives once their kids become teenagers. And they shouldn't be surprised when their latest tech toy becomes part of a tug of war when dividing up their possessions in divorce court.

When the Bubble Shifts to the Other Side

But there's another category of people I've observed at these kinds of gatherings. They find themselves at the other end of the spectrum. They're the folks who have made a deliberate choice to live their lives without any of the high-tech options our modern world has to offer. No cell phones are housed in their pockets or PDAs in their purses. They don't surf the Web because they have no computers on which to "hang ten." There's no Fox News or Weather Channel blinking in the background of their days. No e-mail, no IMs, no text messages in their lives. They pay their bills the old-fashioned way: with a check, an envelope, a stamp, and a hike to the mailbox.

For a small group of people, this makes complete sense. Because of the type of work they do and the fact that no other people in their lives need that technology for their education or personal benefit, they can function comfortably without it. They have no problems with or concerns about all the new technologies—they don't need any of it.

Sometimes the reason people don't have any technology is because they're in the twilight of life. They're old, tired, and ready to move on to their eternal destiny. I am in complete sympathy with their choice to forgo the time and expense needed to work their way up the learning curve of the high-tech world.

But more and more I encounter people on the cusp of what should be their most productive and connected years as a family who have chosen to live their lives with few if any of the high-tech resources that are standard features of the information age. And when I inquire why they've made a choice to deny their family the benefits these tools of tomorrow offer, I usually hear a variation of the same reasons: they don't want to be held hostage by the attention these features would demand of their time, and they don't want to get caught in any of the moral traps often hidden inside.

What a shame. With this decision, these people are denying technology the option of empowering them to be more strategically and *redemptively* connected to their greater world. They're also denying themselves the countless benefits technology has to offer when it comes to helping people lead far more efficient, effective, and informed lives.

And they're doing it for all the wrong reasons.

Let's Hear It for the Digital Age

The Internet and the countless high-tech options the average person has available today deserve our respect and appreciation. Name any dimension of society, and it's easy to see how modern technology has improved our way of life. Be it medicine, missions, or the military; entertainment or education; the marketplace or the scientific community, the technological explosion has created positive opportunities beyond calculation. We can address life's dilemmas and more quickly activate effective solutions to the world's problems than ever before in history. Remove the computer, the cell phone, the satellite, and the electronic transfer of funds from the equation, and then let a massive tsunami hit some remote part of the world. Be prepared to watch the bodies of the innocent pile far higher and relief come far more slowly than it would have without these now-basic necessities.

And that's just one of the *millions* of benefits our little houses on the Internet have going for them.

Has technology also brought an equal amount of negative factors with it? Of course. But that's always been the nature of progress. Every good idea can be appropriated in an evil or corrosive way. In spite of the negative potential, should we deny ourselves the benefits of progress simply because there's a downside to it?

Many would say, "Absolutely!" Unfortunately, that conclusion could set a family up to be destroyed by the very things they fear.

Which brings up the other concern I have about people who choose—out of alarm and distress—not to appropriate the primary pillars of technology into their overall lives. Spiritual logic dictates that people who spurn technology because of its negative potential actually put themselves and their children in the same fragile position as the out-of-balance father on the cell phone at his son's birthday party.

Both types of people are refusing to live a *balanced* life when it comes to their technological options. Balance is available to anyone who chooses to rely on God's power when it comes to controlling the negative effect technology could have. People who reject technology's benefits because they fear its liabilities are choosing to stay in a weak position spiritually. In the process they're actually living lives formatted by the toxic power of technology—rather than the unlimited power of God's Spirit to make wise choices. Besides the negative impact this fear-based strategy has on them personally, they're also modeling this anemic response to technology to their kids, which just about guarantees that their kids will someday find themselves at the mercy of technology rather than in control of it. It's also one of the surest ways to set our children up to be drawn into some of technology's darkest corridors.

I hear people's concerns. They say, "Many of the cable packages come with a lot of toxic movie channels." So remove those premium channels from your order. Cable companies do this for their customers all the time. They come back at me with, "Yes, but even the basic cable package has many despicable programs." I agree. So don't go to those channels—or block them.

You can learn to make decisions empowered by the Spirit of the God of the universe, or you can choose to stay weak and lame. Unfortunately, that second option puts you and your children at the mercy of the very things you fear. What happens when your kids are over at a friend's house or at college and have unbridled access to all of those channels? I hear the comeback: "We taught them God's truth and verses from the Bible about keeping their minds clean." Sorry, but it doesn't work that way. Information, no matter how truthful or biblical, is little more than *information* when implanted into someone's head. It becomes an authentic virtue only when it is trained into a person's heart by the crucible of real life.

"But, Tim, kids can text message all kinds of vile things on their cells, and there are so many inappropriate exchanges when they IM each other." Let me remind you that kids don't need these technological options to communicate inappropriately. They can do it just as easily the old-fashioned way: face to face. Since the Garden of Eden, parents have been given the job of teaching their children how to communicate with reverence and respect for others. We don't get to skirt around our responsibility of transferring these skills to our kids just because someone came up with a high-tech way of doing it.

Ever since someone mouthed the first cussword, God has assigned parents the job of showing their kids how to sift through the detrimental banter that often clutters the lives of people committed to being the salt of the earth. The best way to protect our children from these things is to teach them how to harness the infinite power of God's presence in their hearts to do the right thing—whether it's refusing to respond in kind, or choosing to stay out of chat rooms, or gravitating toward different friends, or ignoring and deleting harmful text messages.

"Oh, but Tim, the Internet is cluttered with millions of miles of back alleys that contain the most hedonistic and pornographic images known to man."

Don't go down those alleys—and teach your kids how to appropriate God's power to resist the urge to go down them too. And when they happen to get drawn to the Internet's negative side, use God's grace, mercy, and forgiveness to help them find their way out.

Obviously there's a time and place for Internet filters in a high-tech family. Especially in your kids' earlier years, before they've made the decision to make Jesus a personal part of their lives. Too often an Internet filter is the main, and sometimes only thing parents do to protect their children—or themselves. That's because they're assuming that the problem is the Internet.

It's not.

The problem is in the child's (or parent's) inability to make wise choices when using the Internet. Otherwise how do you explain this? Millions of people use the Internet every day without the benefit of filters and aren't the least bit enticed by its morally toxic sites. What's their secret? It's not a secret; it's God's basic plan for all of us to maintain calm, confident, and rested lives in the midst of a world of distractions and temptations. It's the simple idea of relying on the power of God within us to make wise choices.

God calls us to instill that power in our children over the duration of childhood. The best way for them to gain this ability is not from lectures but from our example, modeled under pressure. Our kids need to see us defaulting to God's power for victory when we are weak, when the pull of the world, the flesh, or the devil is intense. Our transparent walk through our struggles as well as theirs will do far more than a piece of software ever could.

If all we do is put an Internet filter on the computer, we've only made it tougher for children to act on their curiosity or urges. We've simply postponed the time when they'll be drawn into its dangerous web. Until we have graciously walked with them through the ups and downs of learning how to handle the Internet with moral nobility, we've really done little to equip them to live balanced lives.

What I'm sharing here is a logical argument for true victory and genuine rest. We put fences around our swimming pools and child locks on the cupboards. But our ultimate job is to teach our children how to swim and how to use medicine and cleaning products properly. Once we've done that, they'll know what to do should they fall in the pool or gain access to the cupboards' contents. In the same way, the best method for keeping our kids safe from the dangers of the Internet is to teach them how to use its many benefits properly.

God actually weighed in on this. There is no age restriction on this passage. It applies to both parents and children:

> Consider it pure joy, my brothers, whenever you face trials of many kinds, because you know that the testing of your faith develops perseverance. Perseverance must finish its work so that you may be mature and complete, not lacking anything. (James 1:2–4)

And while we're getting God's perspective on this, listen to what He said about man-made solutions to our fears. In Colossians 2:20–3:3, Paul wrote:

> Since you died with Christ to the basic principles of this world, why, as though you still belonged to it, do you submit to its rules: "Do not handle! Do not taste! Do not touch!"? These are all destined to perish with use, because they are based on human commands and teachings. Such regulations indeed have an appearance of wisdom, with their self-imposed worship, their false humility and their harsh treatment of the body, but they lack any value in restraining sensual indulgence.
>
> Since, then, you have been raised with Christ, set your hearts on things above, where Christ is seated at the right hand of God. Set your minds on things above, not on earthly things. For you died, and your life is now hidden with Christ in God.

Technological Equilibrium

Which leads us to one final group of people at the party. They have the same cell phones and PDAs as the yapping father. They have big business deals they're working on, and powerful people have their numbers. They have the same needs to keep informed regarding their greater world. But they subordinate these realities to a much higher priority: a boy turning three who deserves their undivided attention. They know there's a time to talk on their cell and a time to shut it off. There's a time to respond to e-mail and a time to ignore it—regardless of who it's from. There are appropriate places to visit on the Internet, and there are places that are little more than traps for fools.

They choose carefully.

They know there's a time for a family to go on vacation with a DVD entertaining the kids in the backseat while others sit in their own little iPod worlds. These same people know that there's a time to shut off all these devices, take in some scenery, and connect with one another as a family.

It's called *balance*. And when we're factoring in our children, it's called *parenting*. It's what happens when we let authentic values and seasoned grace guide our everyday choices. The good news is that this option is available to any person willing to let God arrange his or her priorities for a rested and calm life. And what are those priorities? They're the ones we just outlined in the last six chapters:

- A forgiving spirit
- Living within the limits
- An eternal perspective
- Serving while suffering
- Managing your expectations
- Managing your strengths

Regardless of what anyone says to the contrary, you can actually live rested and peaceful lives while enjoying all the advantages of cutting-edge technology.

Virtues: Hollow or Authentic?

Therefore, when it comes to technology, what's the best posture for a family wanting to enjoy rest and calm? To balance technology from their lives or to banish it entirely? It's a critical decision. One offers genuine rest; the other sets us up to live at the mercy of our insecurities. Either you decide to control technology or you surrender to its control over you—even if you never go near it.

One choice requires appropriating the presence and power of God in your life to make wise choices when it comes to technology. The other requires consistently removing access to the problem. One appropriates the power of God's amazing grace. The other is little more than sin management. One claims a true victory by weighing the negative options that technology brings to the table but choosing a virtuous path instead. The other claims a lame victory simply because it has no way of accommodating its internal weaknesses.

One can be incorporated any time, any place, for as long as you live. The other only works as long as the conditions of isolation and denied access can be maintained. Parents who choose this isolated path for raising their kids often pride themselves on their children's virtuous lives. But these are *hollow* virtues. The only reason their children avoid the traps of the Internet and cyberworld is because they have no other choice. They couldn't access it even if they wanted to. Adults who choose this path for their kids eventually find themselves outgunned by the universal presence and sheer power of technology's salvos.

Kids who are equipped on the *inside* with the power and presence of God exercise *authentic virtues*. They avoid the pitfalls of technology by personally choosing appropriate paths and avoiding inappropriate ones. They allow the Creator of the world to be the master of their technological universe. These are people who are keenly aware of the temptations around them and deeply honest with themselves about their own inability to resist these taunts without God's help. They place themselves in His care and call on Him for power in moments of crisis. The more they do it, the stronger they get and the easier it becomes for them to resist the negative features within their technological world.

For the ones with the hollow virtues, it's just a matter of time before they find themselves easily sucked into the most dangerous back alleys of cyberspace. I've seen far too many people from these highly restrictive environments demonstrate little to no willpower when they finally come face to face with Internet porn because they were never shown how to claim the spiritual horsepower that God's Spirit wants to put behind their choices.

Maintaining Rest in a World That Keeps Time in Nanoseconds

We've been to a birthday party. We've met three categories of people. We've established that God offers us power to live calm and well-paced lives even with a wireless card installed in the side of our head. But we can't be naive about the overarching challenges our Internet lives pose to our families. Even without the obvious threat of the shadowy parts of our digital age, other factors must be addressed if we want to maintain equilibrium in our hearts.

If you'll allow me, I'd like to look at a laundry list of challenges that come directly from the various bells and whistles of modern technology.

Technology: It Can Distract Us from Each Other

We pounded this point home fairly well with our visit to the birthday party. But there are a lot of ways short of barking on a cell phone that are far more subtle but equally prevalent. For instance, leaving televisions on in the background. It's not uncommon to find people who keep a news channel on every waking hour of their day. These broadcasts hold people's attention by maintaining nonstop coverage of late-breaking nightmares. They repeat these same reports over and over throughout the day. It's very difficult to maintain a rested heart with a constant stream of crises slipping in the back door of our brains every waking hour.

The same goes for iPods, video games, and texting, which put us inside private little worlds when we're supposed to be participating in a family function designed to connect us to each other's hearts. Love requires eye contact. Grace depends heavily on focused attention. We'd all be a lot better off if we had deliberate times each day when we limited technology's access to ourselves and our access to it.

Speaking of teenagers, nothing is more nerve-racking than watching your son or daughter work on a term paper at the computer while simultaneously listening to downloads, watching a streaming video in a lower-corner window, and maintaining an ongoing IM dialogue with four friends. Card-carrying members of the former generation tend to view this new way of doing homework as "Unacceptable!" simply because it looks like it couldn't possibly be effective. They assume that it would take a grade-A miracle to produce anything remotely close to quality homework. Truth is, the average young person, however, is actually very comfortable with media multitasking, but there is obviously reason for concern.

When it comes to multitasking devices, evidence is clear:

> Social scientists and educators are just beginning to assess their impact, but the researchers already have some strong opinions. The mental habit of dividing one's attention into many small slices has significant implications for the way young people learn, reason, socialize, do creative work and understand the world. Although such habits may prepare kids for today's frenzied workplace, many cognitive scientists are positively alarmed by the trend…. Decades of research (not to mention common sense) indicate that the quality of one's output and depth of thought deteriorates as one attends to ever more tasks.[12]

These conditions can also exacerbate the built-in problems some children already have with learning.

In situations like this, remember one important fact: you're the parent. Don't be afraid to exercise your authority to create conditions that are far more conducive to efficient study and higher-quality homework.

Technology: It Can Possess Our Focus

There's an addictive nature to technology. Video games, e-mail, and the almost stupor-inducing nature of wandering aimlessly through the halls and malls of cyberspace is something everyone must monitor. The average kid spends six and a half hours a day using electronic media.[13] Between television, e-mail, and talk radio, parents aren't far behind. It's not that any of these things are inherently bad, but deep relationships require undistracted time, attention, and focus. Internal rest cries out for corridors of calm in our day.

We'd all do better if we drove home in a quiet car a few days a week, didn't turn on our televisions except when there was something we definitely wanted to see, and made sure that our computers didn't get more of our interest than the members of our family.

Technology: It Can Manipulate and Control Our Behavior and Thinking

You know that technology has you hypnotized when you get up in the middle of the night to use the bathroom and check your e-mail before you climb back into bed. Between cell phones and handheld computers, some people's lives are completely owned and operated by a couple of microprocessors they can carry in a coat pocket.

These things have the power not only to control the way we act but also to manipulate the way we think. Many people choose to get their news from a list of blogs they read every day. These sites ooze opinion that often masquerades as fact. People who refuse to maintain checks and balances with technology can easily find themselves driven to radical mood swings and irrational conclusions in their personal convictions.

Technology: It Can Substitute for Parenting

There's nothing wrong with letting our kids watch a little television, but there's a lot wrong with letting our kids watch television any time they want. Every technology has a legitimate use, but used excessively and as a substitute for parental involvement, these same things can work against our children's academic success, their sibling interaction, and their sense of respect for adults.

More and more parents are using technology like cough syrup on a whiny child. It preoccupies, soothes, calms, and absorbs kids while giving Mom and Dad prolonged breaks from the heavy lifting that goes with parenting. Technology is supposed to be an asset *to* us, not a substitute *for* us.

Some Dos and Don'ts Regarding Technology

- Do take advantage of the many benefits technology offers—especially when they can be used to enhance your relationships with the people you love.
- Don't stand in condemnation of every new invention that comes along. Today's threatening new device is tomorrow's lifesaving necessity. Besides, consistent disapproval of technology makes us appear irrelevant and out of touch to our children.
- Do try things that might seem out of your league (but in your kids'). Download music, send e-mails while walking down a street, IM somebody, put photos of your family members on a memory stick and carry it around with you, text message your grandkids.

- DON'T let technology steal your family and friends. Talk face to face with each other, keep a great adventure going within your family, and cherish the tender moments (waking up, bedtime, the heights of joy, the depths of sorrow). Make sure that each day has generous pockets of quiet away from the white noise of technology.

- DO require cyber manners. No ignoring each other in favor of staying transfixed on the computer screen. No computer games while people are talking to each other. No cell phones at the dinner table. Set limits and create accountability. Online access in the privacy of a teenager's bedroom is a moral kidnapping waiting to happen. Kids are much better off if the only way they can access the Internet is within earshot and eyeshot of other family members.

- DON'T ignore your own bad habits. Adults abuse the computer and television as much as kids do. Personal touch requires that Mom and Dad set the pace by monitoring and minimizing their own use of technology.

- DO ask God for help in maintaining technological equilibrium.

Can You Hear Me Now?

A popular campaign for a cell phone service has branded the pithy question, "Can you hear me now?" into the cortex of a generation of cell phone users. It's a good query to consider when you think about it coming from your spouse, your kids, or your friends. Technology can either help you hear each other's hearts better or it can create a bad connection between you when not kept under control.

If you really want to guarantee that technology is kept in balance, just make sure you can always say yes when you hear God asking that same question: "Can you hear Me now?" So much of our concern about technology and our desire to keep it in balance is contingent on maintaining an intimate, daily connection with the heart of God. A songwriter once referred to the heart of God as a place of "quiet rest." The Lord has given us plenty of leadership when it comes to living well-paced and well-connected lives—even in the middle of the biggest technological revolution in history. You don't have to e-mail Him and then wait for a reply. You don't have to comb the endless back roads of the Web to figure out what's on His mind. He's close, He's personal, He's told us everything we need to know, and He's ready to lead us safely through the digital maze.

Lullaby

When I switched off the desk lamp and tucked my computer in for the night, it was just shy of 1:00 a.m. For the past two hours, I had been sitting at my keyboard, giving instructions to the mainframe computer at my bank on how to disperse my latest paycheck to the vendors and lenders that serve my family. All of the checking and savings accounts had been reconciled, and the values of various investments updated. I was tired but content as I moved toward the stairs to head down to the first floor of our home and go to bed.

But as I turned to go down the stairs, I hesitated. The upstairs of my home was blanketed in the murky shadows of nighttime. A tiny light glowed from the corner of the great room enough to illuminate the half-opened doors to the two upstairs bedrooms. They were the nocturnal addresses of my two middle children, a son and a daughter.

If I were standing a little closer to those doors, I'd be able to pick up the deep and steady breathing of my son asleep in the room on the right and my daughter lost in her dreams in the room on the left. That is, of course, if they were there. But a university in a state twelve hundred miles away had drawn my son to a college apartment a couple of years earlier. And my daughter had started her adventure at a different college a few years after him.

For eighteen years of their lives, I had always been able to slip by their rooms at moments like this, listen to them sleep for a while, and then kiss them good night. But now that option only happened in brief little sound bites in late December and a couple of weeks each summer. They were gone for now and most likely for good…as their wanderings, their work, and their weddings pulled them further and further from the home that had launched them on their respective journeys.

I slipped down the stairs thinking about the years and years of nighttimes my wife and I had taken advantage of to build a sense of calm and rest into their hearts. When the first one was born, there were no computers in our home or cell phones in our pockets. In the brief two decades these kids had lived on the earth, our family had watched technology and international terror completely redefine our world. And as we moved along through each new challenge, my wife and I asked God to show us how to maintain perspective—and turn these changes into opportunities.

My two university students were as technologically savvy as any two young people needed to be. But the confidence they carried with them and the success they were enjoying had little to do with microchips and software. So much of the peace and purpose in their lives came from the presence of Jesus in their hearts. They both loved Him and trusted in His goodness to get them through the busy clutter of their days.

One thing my wife and I did for our kids as they were growing up helped undergird the faith we had worked to build into their hearts. We stopped by their rooms each night to wish them well, pray for them, and then serenade them to sleep. We kept singing them songs every night up through their twelfth birthdays, and after that we just stopped by for prayer and a few tender words. From their first night in our lives through their twelfth year, they heard the first verse of three simple songs sung to them as a lullaby—simple songs from Sunday school that reminded them of how much God loved them and how safe they were in His care. It was the exact message we wanted on their hearts each night as they brought their busy days to an end and slipped off to sleep.

This particular night, being as late as it was and with time zone differences, I assumed that both were deep in sleep by now. But I wished so much that I could sing them those same three songs one more time as they drifted off to sleep.

That's when I saw my cell phone. It weighed only a couple of ounces, but it could easily connect me to these two people I loved so much and missed so badly. Ah, but it was late and I didn't want to disturb them. By now they most likely were slipping into the deeper recesses of their dream cycles. Yet it would be nice to at least let them know I was thinking about them and perhaps remind them again of how much they were loved.

An idea hit me. I could text them a message that wouldn't disturb their sleep. I flipped open my phone, pushed the button for a text message, coded in their cell phone numbers, and then tapped them this message:

> *Jesus Loves Me*
> *Oh, How He Loves You and Me*
> *Silent Night*
> *Good night, Dad*

These were the three songs Darcy and I had sung as their serenade each night. At least my kids could see them in the morning when they got up.

But it turns out they weren't asleep. I barely got into my bedroom when I heard my phone chime that I had an incoming message. And about ten seconds later it chimed again.

I went out to the kitchen, flipped open my phone, and scrolled down to the inbox of my message center.

Thanks, Dad. I love you. Cody

And just below it:

Thanks, Daddy. I love you. Good night. Shiloh

I don't know about you, but I LOVE technology! As far as I'm concerned, "All is calm, all is bright."

BRINGING REST TO YOUR MARRIAGE

My wife and I derive a great deal of joy from exploring the dusty and cluttered back rooms of antique stores. We have a way of sniffing out the best ones in town. To us they're a collage of history and a market of memories. When you live in an age where today will be obsolete by tomorrow, it's nice to visit an era when days lingered for decades. People weren't in that big of a hurry to see what was around the next corner. They were better at taking the time to enjoy where they were.

Because I'm usually ready to join my generation in a race to see what's around the next corner, these visits to antique stores serve as a kind of therapy for me. If the retailers of history aren't outrageous in their pricing, I occasionally bring some of these memories home.

I passed up one item in a store not long ago. I wish now I had purchased it.

One rainy afternoon in central California, I explored an antique shop that was more like the personal museum of a single family. The proprietor must have purchased the entire estate of this family to establish his business. Many of the items bore the monograms or names of the movers and shakers of this home. They had enjoyed their zenith years between the 1880s and the 1920s. One item from the collection made a touching but sad statement about the couple that sat at the apex of this family tree. It was their wedding album.

You've probably seen one of these Victorian albums. The brocade cloth stretched over the padded outer cover was faded from age. The dozen leaves inside had been edged in gold. A century's worth of handling, however, had rubbed away all but a trace of it. Only three pictures of the original collection remained.

In the first, the bride and groom had posed for their formal portrait. They were both sitting in straight-back chairs with blank expressions on their faces. About a foot of empty space was between the two chairs. The new couple wasn't touching each other.

The second picture was a solo portrait of the new bride. She appeared to be in her late teens. Her eyes carried a look of caution and fear. They betrayed the anxiety she no doubt felt about the approaching first night of her honeymoon, but they also seemed to reflect a concern for the mysteries that lay ahead in life for her and her new husband. These first two pictures were traditional poses I've seen in many old albums.

The next few leaves were missing the photos that normally carried images of in-laws and siblings. But the last leaf took me by surprise. It was a break from tradition—a picture you would expect to see in a modern wedding album, but one that seemed out of place and out of character in one assembled over a hundred years ago. The fading photograph captured a glimpse of the celebration and joy that must have pervaded this wedding reception so long ago. The groom was standing with one arm around the waist of his new bride and the other holding a champagne glass high above his head. The bride had replaced her sober portrait look for a full-toothed laugh. Surrounding them were a half-dozen friends who had raised their glasses to toast the young couple's future.

As I gazed at the photo, I was sitting in a rocking chair that had been part of this couple's collection since early in their marriage. They had probably rocked their children through infancy and a few thunderstorms in this chair. If it could talk, this chair would probably tell a lot of anecdotes about the girl behind the laugh and the man who held her close. The chair had watched this laughing young bride with sparkling eyes and shiny hair grow gray and old, and it had helped the anxious groom through a few sleepless nights. Now all the earthly memories of this couple were collecting dust in the corner of an antique shop at the end of a road in California.

One thought kept occupying my mind as I stared at the picture of these newlyweds. They were now dead. The physical remains of these two people who once lived and loved were probably lying side by side in some overgrown cemetery. Their wedding album and their possessions apparently didn't carry much value for the generations they had sired. But fading on the back leaf of the album was evidence that they had once married and had once laughed.

From the quality of their furniture, they must've done all right. From the look of the stamps on their trunk and the curios collected during their travels around the world, they must have enjoyed years of adventure. From the look of everything, this couple that laughed at their wedding must have done a lot of laughing during their walk through time together. Although they were dead, in my mind part of them was very much alive.

A couple weeks after I visited the antique store, I was driving down a street not far from my home. I had my oldest daughter with me, and she was carefully fulfilling her role as "garage-sale lookout." She watched for signs nailed to telephone poles or taped to boxes that gave directions to some front yard flea market.

"There's one, Daddy!"

I slowed down to read the sign.

Garage Sale
GETTING DIVORCED
Everything Must Go!

We followed the signs to the house, parked the car, and walked up the driveway. The various items for sale had been placed in neat rows on each side of the driveway with a four-foot aisle separating them. The gal operating the sale had taken a piece of chalk and written a revealing message on the concrete aisle: HIS STUFF (with an arrow pointing left) and MY STUFF (with an arrow pointing right).

Just about everything a young couple would need to start up house-keeping was there: dishes, linens, cookware, stemware, even a washer and dryer. Sitting on the middle of a card table on the right side of the driveway was an eight-by-ten-inch gold frame holding a wedding picture of the young couple.

They too had laughed.

The young girl running the sale didn't look as if she had changed much in the few years since the picture was taken—except for the laugh. It had been replaced by a seasoned look of contempt. She told me to make her an offer on the frame; she was in a mood to bargain. I asked if she wanted the picture. She gave me a cynical look and said she'd throw it in at no extra charge. I decided this was one picture frame I could live without.

That laughing couple in the eight-by-ten-inch frame was very much alive, but their marriage was dead. The young couple with whom I shared a memory in an antique store one rainy afternoon was dead, but their marriage had been full of life.

What Makes the Difference?

What causes two marriages to start out with the same intentions but end in such different ways? Since I didn't know either couple personally,

I can't really answer this question for them. Nevertheless, the end of one couple illustrates a universal truth, and the end of the other illustrates a universal dilemma.

Most of us who are married laughed in front of the camera at our wedding. We probably laughed for the few days that followed it too. But the frustrations and pressures that begin stalking a new couple at the wedding altar don't take long to make their presence known. The ability to maintain a marriage commitment becomes a challenge—a challenge this hurried era doesn't give us much help with. Our culture punishes those who attempt to endure. When the battle of the bedroom gets too intense, it makes throwing in the monogrammed towel as easy as possible.

We all know divorce is bad news. Those who have endured it would be the first to share how painful and emptying the breakup of a love partnership can be. The generation that is now approaching marrying age fights the inclination to become disillusioned. They want to believe marriage can work, but it's so difficult to find adequate role models.

That's because married couples are forced to row against a strong and contrary current of culture. They find the love that brought them to the altar threatened by the distractions of their struggles and the demands of their successes. They find that the biggest challenge of having a dog, an SUV, and a couple of kids is keeping the whole group together long enough to steal a few laughs.

Not all marriages are hurting, mind you, but it's hard to find one that isn't hassled. Hurried living does that to you. The most conscientious couple can find their commitment tested just because they have too many legitimate responsibilities competing for the time it takes to maintain a healthy relationship.

The average couple these days is deluged with more information than they know how to interpret or assimilate. But if they want to stay competitive in a world that waits for no one, they must try. Information demands choices, work arenas demand action, children demand attention, and the marriage gets whatever energy remains.

Only a few couples come to this rat race with a clue of what they're up against. The parents who reared their children in the 1950s and '60s could never have anticipated the extent of the pressure that would greet their grandchildren when they walked down the aisle on the front side of the twenty-first century. It's easy to see why so many contemporary couples have a difficult time coping. Their best intentions are up against a lot of competition. That probably explains why some couples counter with extreme measures that they hope will bring solutions.

I meet a lot of these types of people in my travels—those who have killed their television, moved to the mountains, and are educating their children themselves. I both admire and respect their decisions. Some of them are doing an excellent job of combating the destructive pressures on their marriages and children.

But most couples simply can't afford the luxury of isolation. And to suggest, as some do, that this sort of withdrawal is a realistic plan for the masses falls far short of practical reasoning. Furthermore, isolation assumes that the problem is environmental. There's no question that our contaminated culture pounds its pressures home every day we're exposed to it. But the biggest determining factor for a successful marriage is not the environment in which the marriage functions but the *attitude* within the hearts of the couple.

Most marriages develop the ability to win the battle against culture by facing it head-on. Pressures won't diminish in the future. We're all guaranteed that the battle for our commitments will increase.

Since most couples will live in the mainstream of life, they need an effective strategy. There are specific actions a couple can take to bring a little sanity back to the middle of the rat race. I've listed 101 suggestions in the appendix, but in this chapter I want to concentrate on the *attitudes* behind the actions.

I'm convinced that the biggest part of the battle for our love is fought between our ears. It can be complicated by outside pressures, but if the attitudes and conditions within our hearts aren't right, our marriage is doomed regardless of outside forces.

In other words, successful marriages don't require certain external conditions in order to be successful. Some of the greatest marriages in history were maintained amid worst-case scenarios. War, imprisonment, separation, famine, poverty, and sickness don't stop committed people from maintaining their love. They are merely factors that must be dealt with as two people who deeply care for each other face the world together.

That's the good news for hurried marriages. The necessities for a secure relationship aren't dependent on life treating us a certain way. We don't have to assume that the tensions of hurried living will get the best of us. In fact, we can approach the mysteries that lie in the future with complete calm—and I'll even take it a step beyond that. We can actually *look forward to* the complications and competition that will confront married couples in the future.

To do this, however, we need a perception of what love is, an understanding of what love requires, and a commitment to carry out those requirements. We all know that this is easier to discuss than implement. Love is always easier to deal with in an abstract way. It's when we get down to the daily responsibilities of living out our understanding of love that we tend to run into problems. That's why we need to be certain in our hearts that we're sure of what we mean when we say the three words the future of civilization rests on: "I love you."

What We Learn from Culture

If we depend on popular culture to help us arrive at an understanding of love, we're probably going to experience some unnecessary heartbreak in life. It's no wonder. The messages about love spewed forth from our culture leave us as bewildered as ever. We live out *the days of our lives* as *the young and the restless,* realizing that we only have *one life to live,* and *as the world turns,* we search for that *guiding light* that will keep us from falling in love at a *general hospital.*

You can see I'm having a bit of fun with the old daytime TV schedule that I grew up with. But the bizarre definitions of love portrayed to millions on daily soap operas or their evening equivalents are no laughing matter. Like heat at a fruit stand, these television dramas exacerbate the decay at the core of our cultural values.

Lest you think I'm beyond being hooked, let me describe an incident on a vacation I took back when our children were still young. My wife and I were visiting some friends at their summer home in Wyoming. A blue-ribbon trout stream snaked its way through the woods and along the fields next to their house. It was irresistible. Whenever the fish were biting, I wanted to be in my waders, working my way upstream.

One morning I came back to the house with a basketful of fish and found no one there to view my trophies! My friend was still fishing farther up the stream, Darcy and the kids had gone to town for groceries. There's nothing more frustrating than looking forward to applause for something I'm only marginally gifted at and ending up with nothing. I'd been skunked the day before, so I figured they would go crazy.

Depression. I decided to nurse my disappointment by turning on the tube. If I couldn't have fish tugging on my line or my wife using her eyes to form an exclamation point as I pulled the fish from my basket, then I was going to fill my time trying to outwit game show contestants.

Because we were so far out in the country, the reception on the television was limited to only a couple stations. Each was broadcasting a soap. It had been some time since I'd watched one of these shows, and they had become a lot more explicit than I remembered! The people on the one I watched had more problems in an hour than I want in my entire life. They said the word *love* a lot but practiced deception, betrayal, anger, and selfishness. I figure this is what the world would be like if only spoiled brats were allowed to fall in love. Everyone took turns either hurting someone or getting hurt.

I couldn't believe anyone would actually watch such a foolish portrayal of life. But the next day I made sure I was out of the stream and in the armchair in time to pick up where all those selfish, brokenhearted people had left off the day before. Within three days, I was addicted. By the end of the vacation, I had a new appreciation for fish. I used to think they were stupid to swallow a lure masquerading as a meal. Yet I had done the same thing. Fortunately I made it through withdrawal by the time I returned home and resisted the urge to take out a subscription to *Soap Opera Digest*.

People actually take these shows seriously, and sometimes their acceptance borders on extreme. A pastor friend told me about a lady in his church who had actually requested prayer for one of the couples on her favorite soap. That's like saying Barney Rubble from *The Flintstones* is a great actor. When we can't separate fiction from reality, we're in trouble.

I know people (lots of them) whose lives seem scripted by soap writers. They approach love without a clue as to what it is. Their lives are young…and restless…and unsatisfied. They keep looking for love in all the wrong places. They are living proof that people are buying the myths about love being fed to us by magazines, television, and movies.

Some of you are old enough to remember the 1970s definition of love popularized by the movie *Love Story:* "Love means never having to say you're sorry." It looks nice on a key chain or written in cursive across a poster of the stars, Ryan O'Neal and Ali MacGraw. But if you use this as a guideline for a relationship, you'll probably find yourself sorely disappointed. That's because love means *always* having to say you're sorry (sometimes even when you haven't done anything wrong). When a person lets a loved one down, he or she should assume responsibility for it.

Our culture throws tremendous interference and static at a married couple trying to fine-tune their love, which makes it unusually difficult to arrive at accurate conclusions about this mysterious need inside all of us. That's why we must be careful not to allow culture to be an outspoken authority on the subject.

What We Learn from Experience

Culture vies for a big part in forming our view of love. But its impact is minimal next to the power of experience. What we learn from being loved or being rejected builds the strongest foundation beneath our concepts of love. But here again we run into problems. If experience is our teacher, then we are at the mercy of many variables beyond our control. The parents who reared us, the neighbors who surrounded us, the teachers and religious mentors who influenced us, and the treatment we received in the hands (or the arms) of the people we allowed close to us provide the often conflicting and confusing impressions that make up our understanding of love.

We arrive at the marital altar with a lot of these experiences having created conflicting attitudes. We use the word *love* throughout the wedding ceremony and swear it's the cement bonding our vows. But the married life that follows often reveals that both parties entered into the relationship with their own very personal and inadequate definitions.

Defining Love

The definition of love we bring to marriage has everything to do with whether or not we can experience love now and enjoy it for a lifetime. When I visit with a couple struggling in their relationship, I like to ask them to give me their definition of love. My thinking is that if they understand what love is, they're more inclined to achieve it. What I find in almost every case is that both partners have come to the relationship with only the vaguest notion of what love entails.

Think a minute. If you were asked to write out your definition of love, what would you put down? I know that love is one of those dimensions of life that's hard to put into words, but if we're going to be serious about this aspect of our life, we have to know what we mean when we say, "I love you."

I want to share with you a definition of love that can bring calm to a hurried marriage. It can make the relationship between a husband and wife an oasis in the middle of a thirsty culture. Those who seriously embrace this definition can maintain the ability to love for the duration of their life. If a couple loves with this type of love, they'll never have to hold a "getting divorced" garage sale. They can move beyond today to a lifetime of certainty and contentment.

Let's define love this way:

Love is...
the commitment of my will
to your needs and best interests
regardless of the cost.

This is a definition that doesn't carry with it a bunch of conditions. It doesn't require anything from the person being loved. Instead, it is preoccupied with what we can *give*.

I get a variety of responses when I share this definition with people. Sometimes they say it's exactly the way they would define love. Yet a close examination of their lives shows that what they believe in theory isn't carried out in practice. Others call the definition unrealistic, idealistic, or even impossible.

I agree that it's not a "natural" way to respond to others, but it is very much an achievable standard for a relationship. Couples who use this as their standard need not fear the present or the future. That's because love that is practiced according to this definition is solid. Secure love! Steady, reliable, constant, unshakable, immovable. Isn't that what our hearts long for?

This sort of love is the anchor we throw out when the winds of change shred our sails and the waves of doubt swamp our engines. It's the confidence that comes from being stable in unstable conditions. As marriages throughout America take a fierce beating from culture, couples with secure love can rest in each other's arms. It's this kind of love that turns fear into faith, intimidation into anticipation, worry into wisdom, and failure into success.

As married couples navigate their way toward the future, their love for each other may be the only part of their lives that seems permanent. And if their love is permanent, they can accept the changes life brings their way. *Any* changes.

If your love is secure, you can accept anything.

The Power Behind the Love

We are human. We have weaknesses. We bring fragile needs to our marriage relationships. Loving your spouse by committing your will to meet his or her needs and best interests, regardless of the cost, is *superhuman*. It just isn't the normal, natural way people operate. It's a superhuman form of love that comes from the heart of the supernatural God who made us. If we want to have this kind of love for each other, we must first derive it from God. The husband or wife trying to love without a heart possessed by the Author of love is going to run out of momentum very quickly—more quickly than he or she would have ever imagined.

Love has a bad habit of giving us pop quizzes. When we have only our human resources to draw on, we find ourselves in trouble quickly. We need a source of love that knows no boundaries and has no limits. And a God who would cross the threshold of time, walk down a back street of civilization, and climb up on a cross that was meant for us knows how to help us love.

Secure love, therefore, requires a secure relationship with the God who *is* love. This relationship takes a good definition of love and puts *power* behind it. Infinite muscle. It helps us practice in our lives what we intellectually embrace in our hearts.

The Bottom Line

If we have this divine help, then we can begin to implement three crucial ingredients for successful love. These ingredients are:

1. Self-discipline
2. Self-discipline
3. Self-discipline

Actually, they are *self-discipline, sensitivity,* and *sacrifice.* But if we aren't willing to discipline our commitment to love, then sensitivity and sacrifice won't happen anyway. Finding rest in our marriages takes work. It takes a preoccupied commitment to oneness.

Married life in the passing lane provides the ultimate challenge to self-disciplined love. A typical couple faces an array of choices they must make each day if they want to remain committed. Something is always ready to rob us of our time, someone always willing to wedge between us and divide us. Many of the challenges that face us in marriage are good and rewarding—like raising kids and achieving high levels of financial success—but without self-discipline attached to our commitment, these challenges can produce a chilling effect on our love.

So we must love with a clear conviction of what we mean by *love* and oppose anything or anybody that poses a threat to our marital vows. But even if we win the battle against the external competition, we still must face the problems within us that make having a rested marriage difficult. It might require a complete retooling of our concept of love and a recommitment to our vows.

One thing we can do is decide in advance that we are going to make a *unilateral commitment* to our spouses. In other words, we are going to fulfill our promises *regardless of what our spouse does*. This attitude is not what I hear coming from the weeping wives or hurting husbands who share their pain in counseling. Each has a list of disappointments that serve as the basis for his or her uncommitted behavior. The index finger that points at the errant partner is ultimately connected to a broken heart. As the disappointments build, the ability to maintain love diminishes.

Unilateral love is another way of saying *unconditional love*. It's saying to your partner, "I love you and I'm going to live out this commitment, no matter what." You may be reading this and thinking, *Tim, you're dreaming. I could never do that.* I can appreciate that you may have many painful reasons for thinking that, but I assure you that until you make such a commitment, you won't have a relationship that can bring inner rest.

You may have serious hurts, felonies against your marriage covenant such as infidelity, betrayal, and desertion—hurts that have plagued your relationship in the past. Your reasons for resisting might be strong, but your relationship will never enjoy contentment until you are willing to take the first step of unconditional commitment. You need the same kind of attitude toward your spouse that you have toward your children. Your kids may have disappointed you, betrayed you, or rejected you, but you won't ever stop loving them.

Once you are prepared to commit to your relationship, the six non-negotiables necessary for rest discussed in this book become a simple checklist to keep you on target. Maybe a few examples of how to apply these principles will help you see how to make them personal. Allow me, for our discussion here, to change the order in which they are listed in earlier chapters.

Managing Your Expectations

If there is any one area in a relationship that controls our ability to find inner rest, it is the expectations we bring to our marriage.

Two people stand before the preacher with great expectations. This beautiful, intelligent, bright-eyed young woman stands hand in hand with her strong, courageous, and handsome young man. They are going to enjoy a few busy days and rewarding nights before the honeymoon feelings wear off. It may take a year, a month, or twenty-four hours, but they *will* wear off. That's not so bad. Those who preach that every day can be a honeymoon have either never been married or never been on a honeymoon. Reality is insensitive to the happily-ever-after feelings that fill a couple's heart as they drive from the wedding reception to their first night together.

Reality is going to visit this couple in many ways—job insecurity, credit card bills, old loves, new loves, dirty diapers, late notices, cold dinners, poorly timed affections, poorly timed headaches, bounced checks, and eventually a chest where a stomach used to be and nothing where a chest used to be.

This post-honeymoon period is the time when married couples most need realistic expectations. Unfortunately, these new pressures usually reveal just the opposite.

I'll make this simple. When most of us come to a relationship, we bring a formula for success that assumes our partner will act, think, and respond in certain ways. *That is why so many of us become disappointed with our spouses.* We are expecting that individual to fulfill our own personal formula for happiness, and that's fine if he or she is cooperative. Unfortunately, we marry humans, not robots. We marry people with minds of their own—and their own set of unrealistic expectations!

When our partner doesn't fulfill the expectations of our formula for happiness, we panic. Some people try to muscle their spouse into cooperating with their formula. (This always backfires.) Others give in. Too many give up.

There is a way to counter all of this. It's going to sound far-fetched to a lot of you, but believe me, it's the only way a couple can bring rest to their relationship. Let's shift to the first person to make our point.

What I need to do is come to a relationship with expectations that cover only *me*. After all, I'm the only person over whom I have control. I don't control my wife, and I don't want to. Even if I wanted to, I couldn't. She's an individual with a mind of her own.

Instead of making her actions a requirement for my success, I want to make my actions a commitment to *her* success. In other words, if my contentment is contingent on her cooperation, I'm sure to lack contentment. If, however, my contentment is wrapped up in bringing to my marriage all that I can offer without requiring *anything* in return, I am more likely to enjoy peace in my marriage. I shift my spouse from being the accommodator of my needs to being the true object of my love.

Bringing rest to a distracted and hurried marriage means managing my expectations for the relationship. If my formula for being fulfilled in my love is knowing that I have committed my will to the needs and best interests of my spouse, no matter what the cost, then I can control that. If she doesn't respond in kind, I can still experience the rest that comes from knowing I've done my part. But if she responds with a similar attitude toward me, our marriage is doubly blessed.

A Forgiving Spirit

Marriages can't handle the long-term pressure of bitterness. Husbands and wives hurt each other. Sometimes it's accidental; other times it's premeditated. Regardless, individuals desiring rest in their marriage must be prepared to forgive. They must be willing to crumple up their list of hurts and throw it in the trash can at the foot of the cross.

I know some people can list hurts that seem beyond forgiveness. God can do the same thing when it comes to us. Yet He still forgives us. That's why when it comes to our spouse, forgiveness must come through God's power. It is the only way to put rest and peace where bitterness once festered. It is a gift we can give to our spouses, but it is also a gift we give to ourselves. It means we're willing to do something about the anger in our hearts. In the process of disciplining our love, we bring rest to our spirits as well.

Living Within the Limits

Several years ago, a professor from one of our nation's more respected seminaries was interviewed on an afternoon television talk show. He shared that he enjoyed a great marriage with his wife of twenty-five-plus years. During the conversation, he said that one of the reasons he felt their marriage was strong was because of their sexual relationship. However, when he let the viewing audience peek into the privacy of their bedroom, people were surprised to see that this couple shared their bed and their sexual relationship with someone else.

This theologian was proud of the fact that when they made love, he always brought his latest edition of *Penthouse* to bed with him. He would stretch Miss Whomever out on the bed next to his wife. There was no comparison. The two-dimensional playmate became the real object of his affections. His wife was only there to complete the fantasy. He made love to two women at the same time—the wife in his arms and the airbrushed centerfold in his mind.

This couple was living a lie. This husband was defrauding his wife by not accepting her for who she was. He was only using her while filling his mind with images she could never fulfill.

No marriage can survive without boundaries. Anyone who says otherwise is dreaming. A river without boundaries is a swamp. Swamps stink. A married couple who want security and rest must recognize that there are clear boundaries when they deal with each other. These boundaries aren't there to fence in our freedom but to fence out those pressures, people, and personal policies that would seek to steal it.

A partner who turns to an affair to provide the missing magic is practicing cruel self-deception. Affairs *don't* work. They just appear to work on the front end when the people involved are making their decisions with their emotions…or their hormones. The excitement is transitory—and is soon overwhelmed with emptiness and regret.

When God said don't covet someone else's property, don't commit adultery, and don't steal, He said it because He knew what disciplined love requires. Those who willingly submit their thoughts and actions to the clear boundaries God outlines in the Scriptures say "I love you" in one of the most genuine ways possible.

An Eternal Perspective

Our commitment to each other in marriage is "until death do us part." But even though marriages end, we don't. The soul of an individual is eternal. The apostle Paul told husbands that their responsibility to their wives ends when they die but is realized when they meet the Lord. We are to love our wives and live with them in such a way that they can come to God "holy and blameless" (Ephesians 5:27).

Keeping in mind that the person who sleeps next to you at night and eats across the table from you each day is eternal has a way of changing how you treat that individual. Honoring, affirming, and cherishing become greater priorities when we know he or she can be part of a gift package to God for all eternity.

Serving While Suffering

Sidney would come home from work drained, but three hungry children had to be fed. Over the years he had become fairly efficient. Eager little hands would do a childish job of setting the table while his tired hands worked over the stove. Laughs and lectures would make the dinner ritual more than substance for the body—it was also an investment in a lifetime.

Dishes would be washed, clean pajamas would replace the clothes that bore the marks of the day's adventures, and stories and prayers would help sleepy eyes drift from the cares of the day to the quiet and safety of slumber.

That's when Sidney would retire to the back corner of the house. He'd say good-bye to the day nurse and then complete the rest of his evening ritual. A catheter bag had to be emptied, and a bedpan had to be offered. He would take a clean washcloth and warm water to wash the face of his bride. It had been a couple of years since the accident, yet his vows were clear: *for better or for worse*. It could have been he who was hit by the drunk driver. Instead, it had been the woman he loved.

He would tell her all the good things about his day, never the worries. She loved music, so he'd hum her a few tunes from their past. Then he'd look into her eyes and tell her what he told her every night before she went to sleep and every morning when she woke up.

"I love you, honey. You're my life, my love, and my wife."

He had regrets, sure. But no complaints. Although his life was different and difficult, he could live it with a rested spirit. He understood that rest sometimes requires us to serve when we suffer.

Managing Your Strengths

A married couple in search of rest must learn how to discipline their gifts and assets. The people who make up the marriage—and the children their union creates—represent the greatest treasures of all. We must manage those treasures well.

There is a practical way this works out in a marriage. If a husband is frivolous with his money and slothful with his talent, he makes a statement to his wife. He's saying, "Your security isn't that important to me— *you* aren't that important to me." If a man won't stick with a job and can't keep his checkbook reconciled, he is going to rob his wife of rest.

When a wife who doesn't have to work outside the home neglects the house and doesn't maintain the household possessions, she is saying to her husband, "I don't value what you provide—therefore I don't value who you are."

Our bodies are gifts and assets we gave to each other on our wedding day. Time and gravity will challenge us, but we must not use these as excuses not to do everything within our power to keep ourselves as healthy and fit as possible with the genes God has given us.

Managing the gifts God has given personally and as a couple requires serious discipline. Failure to be conscientious in this area of our relationship is guaranteed to add a lot of disappointment, pain, and restlessness to our marriage.

With the world spinning so fast and friendships so few, a marriage may be the only stable and secure commitment a couple will know throughout their hurried life. Therefore this aspect of the relationship must be a higher priority if a person wants to enjoy rest over the long haul.

John Fischer, a Christian musician, offers some sound advice along these lines. It seems John once rented a room from an elderly couple who had been married longer than most people get a chance to live. But even though time had wrinkled their hands, stooped their posture, and slowed them down, it hadn't diminished the excitement and love they felt toward each other. John could tell that their love hadn't stopped growing since the day of their wedding over a half-century before. Intrigued, the singer finally had an opportunity to ask the old man the secret to his success as a husband.

"Oh, that's simple," the old gentleman said with a twinkle in his eye. "Just bring her roses on Wednesday—she never expects them then."

GIVING THE GIFT OF REST TO YOUR CHILDREN

My everyday life is filled with visual reminders of priorities. The soap-written message scribbled on the bathroom mirror reminds me that I have a breakfast appointment. The stub my wife has wedged into the crease in my steering wheel reminds me that I need to pick up the dry cleaning on the way home from the office. I can't even start my car without it reminding me that I may have an accident and I'd probably be glad that I put on my seat belt.

Something about routine makes us humans prone to forgetfulness. Even though four children have spent the bulk of their lives living under my roof, it's easy to get so distracted by the madness of my daily responsibilities that I forget how much of my attention they need. "Out of sight, out of mind" became a cliché because it's true. Because I spend a lot of the day at my office, it's easy to fall into the trap of making my children a *compartment* of my life rather than its *essence*.

In my desperation to remember my priorities, I set seven individually framed pictures across the back of my credenza at work. The picture on the left is of the Jameson Memorial Hospital in New Castle,

Pennsylvania. That's where I was born. The picture on the right is of a six-foot-high granite monument that stands in the middle of the Graceland Cemetery just outside this same town. You can't miss the word *Kimmel* carved on its side. The earth beneath it conceals the remains of several generations of my family. The five pictures that sit between these two outer pictures are of my wife, Darcy, and my children, Karis, Cody, Shiloh, and Colt.

What we do for a living has a way of absorbing our attention. Its demands are so great and its ego satisfaction so intoxicating that it can easily become the focus of our lives. I love my work, but I don't want it to become the heart of my existence—my reason for living. That's why I have those pictures strategically placed on my desk. When I look up from my studies, I come eye level with a reminder of my purpose. Stealing a peek at them several times a day has a way of keeping my work (and my life) in proper perspective. In the brief moment it takes me to scan them, I receive a message in the cluttered back rooms of my brain. The pictures say, "Don't forget, Tim. *This* is where you checked in (the hospital), *this* is where you're checking out (the cemetery), and *these five people* in the middle are *why you're here.*"

My job as a parent is a temporary responsibility with eternal consequences. The amount of time my wife and I have to adequately develop a sense of inner security and personal adequacy within our children is fleeting. Incredibly brief. They'll only be in our home for about twenty years. And since they are going to sleep, eat, and go to school during most of that time, we need to wisely use the small amount of time left.

But our lives are cluttered with choices and distractions that make giving priority to our children difficult. We need to remind ourselves every day that the time we have to pass on a heritage of rest and calm is quickly dwindling away.

We have to be deliberate about our commitment to them if we ever want to meet their inner needs for secure love, significant purpose, and strong hope. By giving them these gifts, we equip them for life. Children who know they are loved, know they have a purpose, and know they have hope are prepared for anything this world wants to dish up. A rested, well-paced, and loving home is the only environment that naturally satisfies these needs.

As Laurens van der Post and Jane Taylor say in their anthropological study *Testament to the Bushmen,* "No culture has ever been able to provide a better shipyard for building storm-proof vessels for the journey of man from the cradle to the grave than the individual nourished in a loving family."[14]

Secure and loving homes don't just happen. The competition for time and concentration is too intense. If parents want their children to be raised in an environment that produces calm and confidence, they're going to have to pay attention to make it happen.

Priorities for Parenting

Because hurried lives have a way of stealing our attention, we need to make a calculated effort to maintain priorities that will give our children the best possible chance of achieving security, significance, and strength as adults. There are two priorities every parent should be careful not to neglect. Others could be mentioned, but when it comes to giving rest to your children, these are the ones from which you'll derive the most help.

The first priority is *preparation.* We must always keep in mind that our job as parents is to prepare our children to live independently of us. Before they move out from under our influence, they must be adequately prepared to face the best and worst that life might bring their way. There will always be lessons for them to learn as adults, but before they leave our home, the fundamental disciplines of life must be developed enough to allow them to adapt and survive in an adult's world.

If we are to prepare them to leave, we must be prepared to let them go. Too often, adolescent children are prepared to leave, but the parent refuses to cut the cords to set them free. Parents who keep their children in a position of dependence, or who refuse to back out of their lives as the children reach adulthood, do more damage than they could ever imagine.

Once our children get out of college, we need to move from being a *resource* to being a *reference*—we offer advice when solicited. This forces our children to stand on their own two feet. If we indefinitely bankroll them, we keep them in neutral. They need to start stumbling and getting up on their own if we ever expect them to run with the pack.

The following analogy might be a bit worn, but its truth is fresh. When a mother eagle builds her nest, she structures the frame out of thorns and twisted limbs. She pads this thorny nest with down and feathers. As the eaglets hatch and mature, they enjoy the comfort and warmth of their feathered nest. But as they reach maturity, the mother eagle has to take deliberate measures to get them to jump out and fly. That's when she starts to remove the down that pads the nest. The young eagles become more and more interested in flying as the nest gets more and more uncomfortable.

The mother eagle wants her babies to soar to great heights as adults. That's what good parents want for their children. But it will never happen if we don't prepare them for independence.

It's good to communicate this to our children as they grow up. We need to let them know what we're doing and why we're doing it. When they know that instruction and activity in the present are going to serve them in the future, they learn to feel confident. We give them rest because they know we're taking the worry out of growing up and moving on.

When your children are young, simple chores can become excellent opportunities to let them know you are preparing them to be successful adults. If they're helping you cook, you can make them understand that this skill will serve them well when they are out on their own. As you help them clean their rooms, you can encourage them that they're learning how to be good managers of their own homes someday.

Anything you do to prepare them for the future is a way of saying, "I love you." Preparation, then, helps parents meet the requirement of giving rest to their children. But preparation by itself isn't enough. We need a second priority for giving rest to our children.

This is the priority of *protection*.

Life can be harsh on children. When they're young, they are defenseless when it comes to competing with the philosophies and forces within a culture that would seek to harm or mislead them.

Parents play a critical role in protecting their offspring from these cultural pressures. Our job is to run interference for our children, to lead them. They need to know that we will fight the battles they are unprepared to face. They gain inner confidence in knowing we will do the providing, the worrying, and the struggling until they are ready to do it themselves.

All along we are preparing them to be able to protect themselves. These two priorities, then, accommodate each other. We protect them by preparing them, and we prepare them by protecting them.

A Four-Dimensional Checklist

Four different dimensions make up a child's personhood: the *physical* dimension, the *emotional* dimension, the *intellectual* dimension, and the *spiritual* dimension. If we want to do a good job of giving rest to our children, we have to help them in all four dimensions. Batting three-for-four may be great in baseball, but with children it's simply going to leave them unprepared for the future. Children need help in all four areas if they want to enjoy a balanced attitude toward life.

Restlessness has a way of creeping in through the unlocked doors of our personhood. Leaving a child's personality unguarded is an open invitation to frustration, heartache, and pain.

With this in mind, let's think through our four-point checklist. With each dimension, we need to consider how we can both prepare and protect our children so that they can enjoy the maximum amount of calm and confidence on their journey into adulthood.

Rest for the Body

Some kids lack inner rest simply because they lack physical rest. Children don't naturally know how to monitor their energy levels as an adult would. Instead of pacing themselves, they will literally run until they drop. There are times when that's okay. If our children are having a lot of fun playing in the backyard, we may choose to forgo their naps. But we must compensate by putting them to bed early. Children need that kind of supervision to make sure they develop adequate rest habits. A student who works hard in school, overprepares her homework, and maintains a busy social calendar sometimes needs a parent to call time-out. The child needs to be reminded that bodies have limits and that those who push themselves pay too high a price. We cannot assume that the child has thought this through. It may never have occurred to her!

Another area in which parents can play a big role is in a child's diet. Children who aren't taught how to eat properly and maintain their weight are going to struggle all their lives. By not helping our kids in this area, we are setting them up for loads of frustration and anxiety. And the physical difficulties brought on by poor eating habits often prove to be minor compared to the emotional hurts that come with being overweight or extremely underweight.

The bottom line is that we need to help our children make proper choices when it comes to their bodies. It will protect them now and prepare them for tomorrow. In the meantime they will experience the joy of being at rest inside because they have the outside under control.

Rest for the Emotions

I wish there were a way to hook a sign on every kid's chest just above the heart that reads: "Handle with Care—Fragile Emotions on Board." I honestly can't believe how careless some parents are with their children's emotions. They thoughtlessly presume that kids have sophisticated emotions capable of processing input at a mature adult level. They're wrong. Dead wrong! But too often, before they figure it out, the damage has been done.

A parent can crush a child's spirit with a glance or a few poorly chosen words. I've done that. But the fact is that kids' young emotions are delicate, and we need to be careful how we handle them. Since children are a responsibility from God, we are called to steward them well. We will be just as responsible for how we stewarded our children's emotions as for how we stewarded our money.

How can we make sure that we are preparing our children emotionally? There are several ways, but let me mention just a few.

One thing we can do is teach them the purpose of emotions. It is crucial to teach a child that emotions are for *feeling*, not for *thinking*. This may seem obvious, but my experience in counseling is that too many people call on their emotions to do critical thinking. This always leads to trouble because emotions aren't designed for those sorts of demands.

Emotions only know how to feel—and they don't even have to tell the truth. Emotions are free agents. They can feel any way they want. Even irrationally. You might be at a friend's birthday party and not be able to stop crying. You might be at a funeral and not be able to stop laughing. You think you're going crazy when all that is really happening is that you're experiencing the effects of emotions that have a mind of their own.

If we don't teach our children how to recognize the proper use of their emotions, they could be tempted to call on emotions to do their reasoning for them. That's the surest way to create a person plagued by impulsiveness. People who think with their emotions can end up spending their lives fighting problems with debt, divorce, promiscuity, and job instability. In other words, they are guaranteed restlessness.

Our children need to learn how to allow their emotions freedom of expression while avoiding the temptation to use them as the basis for making vital decisions. Our children need to see us pull back from the feelings that surround a major decision long enough and far enough to appraise it objectively. We shouldn't buy big-ticket items on a whim. We shouldn't pass judgment on people with only first impressions. Kids need to see their parents processing life through intellect—the facts, logic, truth, and common sense—as well as emotions.

A second way parents can help give rest to their children's emotions is by giving them the gift of tears. Tears free up a languishing spirit by providing an outlet of relief.

I listened recently to a pastor talking about one of the saddest events in our nation's history. Most people old enough to have watched the funeral of President John Kennedy remember the strength little "John-John" Kennedy showed as the casket of his father lay in front of him. Before he saluted the casket, however, John-John was fighting tears. His little heart wanted to wail. He was informed, however, that he was a Kennedy, and "Kennedys don't cry!"

If Kennedys were born with tear ducts, then Kennedys were meant to cry. Tears can be a companion through the dark hours and a comfort when words and affections fail. Our children, both girls *and* boys, must not be discouraged from crying because crying is a significant way to bring rest to their emotions.

The same can be said for laughter! Smiles and laughter are natural inclinations. But insensitivity and bitterness can wipe the smile off a child's face forever. When we fill our children's days with laughter, we medicate their emotions. We introduce them to an internal friend that will be loyal to them their entire lives.

Another way parents can give rest to their children's emotions is by displaying affection. Children receive more confidence from a hug than they do from a good grade on their report card. They get more mileage out of a compliment than they do out of an expensive store-bought gift. Affection—meaningful touch and affirming words—forms a wall of protection around a child's confidence. It's hard to feel insignificant when a mother and father are generous with their affection.

Meaningful affection is the best way to protect your son or daughter from sexual pressures in the future. A child who is starving for affection is a lot more inclined to succumb to physical temptation than one who regularly receives a meaningful touch and compliments.

Preparing and protecting your child's emotions is also an investment in your grandchildren! Ever thought of that? Stable and secure emotions have a way of reproducing themselves.

Emotions that are guarded and guided by loving parents are emotions that will hold up against an angry world. They are emotions that will enjoy honest expression when they are called on to celebrate at the wedding of a friend, worry at the side of a sick child, or moan over the casket of a mate. Conscientious parenting calls us to give the sweet sense of rest to our children's emotions.

Rest for the Mind

Most parents would say they do a fairly decent job of preparing their children intellectually. That's because we assume that a good education is our child's biggest requirement for intellectual competence.

Unfortunately, a good education only guarantees that a child has mental skills. It says she can compete in the arenas that are branches of her training. But we all know that education doesn't transfer calm. Some of the most educated people who have ever lived make the best case studies for depression and anxiety. Rest is not a product of education.

Parents, on the other hand, can help their children learn how to use their intellect to overcome restlessness. Common sense isn't genetic; it is a skill picked up by observation. When children see us use common sense to solve problems, to overcome prejudice, to choose right and avoid wrong, they feel confidence building inside of them. That's because common sense keeps us out of trouble; it keeps us from living life at extremes. Extremes clutter a life with anger, feelings of superiority, and isolation. People who live balanced lives can find rest and calm more often and more easily.

But commonsense parenting recognizes that even though education doesn't guarantee rest, it does raise the odds for achieving gainful employment. Being able to make a living and compete in the future is going to have a lot of bearing on our children's sense of calm and confidence once they are adults. The high-tech world waiting for the next generation of students to graduate isn't going to be very sympathetic to the unprepared. The adults of tomorrow will have to be able to not only think intellectually but logically.

Parents serious about giving their children intellectual rest must be prepared to help them. Children need coaching, tutoring, and discipline to gain the skills needed to be balanced. Parents who do a thorough job of educating their children have to be committed to sacrifice. The work required to produce intellectual discipline is seldom innate within a child. It has to be developed in each person.

While we're on the subject of intellectual discipline, I observe some parents going to two dangerous extremes. One extreme is that of overachievement. Straight A's, honor roll, dean's list, and awards are overemphasized. Parents may *say* that they only expect a child to do his best, but the child is watching the parents' nonverbal cues too. He knows when his parents have made achievement the key to their affirmation and affection.

Driven, overachieving parents have a bad habit of passing on their bad habits. There is no rest for a driven heart. Kids who pick up these kinds of habits are more likely to spend all the extra money they make from their achievements paying bills at the cardiac care unit or the therapist's office when they're older. Pushing a child toward excellence for the sake of excellence is a betrayal. We need to draw them to do their best, not push them beyond, toward perfection.

The other extreme I see some parents take is focusing a child's intellectual training in one area to the exclusion of others. Some do this because of a particular interest of their own. But others "guard" their child from a broad education because they're afraid of exposing their child's mind to certain myths or lies within a given field of academics.

I agree that children need to be protected from some teachings, but we must be selective in our protection. In their zeal to protect their children, some parents unwittingly leave them ill-equipped to weigh information critically. The unfortunate result is that our children can become trapped by the very myths and lies we were trying to keep them from embracing. A good, balanced exposure to fine arts, literature, history, and science—with a loving parent looking over the child's shoulder—can help resolve this dilemma.

Involved parents can help their children weigh the problem areas of education. Parents who take time to help their children consider potential threats to a developing value system prepare them to stand on their own. Open-minded people are often vulnerable to deception, but closed-minded people can be dangerous as well. What we need are parents who stand for a value system that is grounded in God's unwavering truth and who take the time to transfer it to their child's intellect. That produces balanced children who grow up to make a difference while enjoying rest in crucial areas of their lives.

Rest for the Spirit

The greatest asset parents can give their children is a spiritual heritage. Children need to know they are supremely loved by a personal God. They need to rest in the eternal security found in a personal relationship with Jesus Christ.

I'm shocked how often and how badly parents drop the ball in this area. It's almost as if they don't acknowledge the spiritual dimension's existence.

When I was a youth pastor at my local church, a young man named Calvin came to visit our Wednesday evening Bible study. He was looking for some answers to big questions in his life. You could tell there was a void in his heart that needed to be filled by God.

After visiting for a few weeks, Calvin made a decision to give his life to God. I prayed with him and gave him a Bible. We chatted at length before he went home to tell the good news to his parents.

About eleven o'clock that night, I received a call from an angry mother. She had venom in her voice as she worked me over verbally. She claimed that we were shoving religion down her son's throat—that he was too young to understand how to believe in a God he couldn't see. She further said that she wanted her son to be open-minded, not limited to one concept of God.

After venting her anger, she stopped a moment to catch her breath.

My turn! I thought.

"Excuse me, ma'am, but did you teach Calvin about Santa Claus when he was little?"

The answer was indignant. "Of course I did."

"Did he believe in Santa?"

"Yes."

"So much for the argument that children can't believe in something they can't see. Let me ask another question: Do you think table manners are important?"

"Yes."

"Did you insist on Calvin observing good manners at the table as he grew up?"

"Yes."

"Why?" I asked.

"I wanted him to know how to behave properly at the table."

"Good. That was wise. But you know, I find it interesting that you could be so dogmatic about table manners and yet so threatened when your son becomes concerned about his destiny."

This mother ultimately withdrew her boy from church and discouraged him from pursuing any spiritual heritage. Calvin is in his midforties now. He's failed at marriage and still fights deeply embedded self-destructive tendencies.

People are eternal just as certainly as they are physical, intellectual, and emotional. A parent wouldn't think of withholding food and sleep from his or her child's physical life. Nor would any decent parent deny a child a proper education or the freedom to laugh and cry. Parents recognize that children are intellectual and emotional beings. Yet many parents completely starve and neglect the spiritual dimension of their children's life, as though it doesn't even exist. Not only does it exist, but it is just as real as the physical, intellectual, and emotional dimensions. And the spiritual side of our children is the one dimension that will still exist after the other three cease at their death. Because of that fact, we must not deny our children's legitimate need for eternal answers.

And just as there is junk kids can eat that isn't good for them, incorrect information that could mislead them intellectually, and many ways to mishandle their emotions, there is a right way and a wrong way to help them develop the spiritual dimension of their life. If Satan can't get parents to neglect their children's spiritual life, he does the next worst thing—he gets parents to lead their kids down incorrect spiritual paths. Either way the damage is done. That's why we must not only meet our children's spiritual hunger for forgiveness of sins, a relationship with their Creator, and eternal life, but we must make sure we're presenting the truth accurately.

Thank the Lord for the Bible!

A strong biblical emphasis lived out in the context of a grace-based family is the greatest gift a child could ever receive. It is the gift of rest wrapped in its most beautiful wrapping paper.

Our children need church, the Bible, and prayer from the leadership of parents who embrace these elements themselves. This will provide the main ingredient needed for completing the physical, emotional, and intellectual dimensions of their life—*the truth*. Jesus said, "You will know the truth, and the truth will make you free" (John 8:32, NASB).

Preparation for Life's Front Lines

One young man knows the power that can be found in a Christian heritage. Dr. Billy Kim, a leading minister from South Korea, shared a powerful story that came from the shadows of one of Korea's darkest hours.

Heartbreak Ridge stretches east to west along the thirty-eighth parallel dividing North and South Korea. The ridged rocks making up this mountain range look like gigantic shark's teeth from a distance. The mountain got its name from the battles that were fought near its peak. During the Korean War, Heartbreak Ridge was bathed in the blood and tears of thousands of Korean, American, and UN soldiers.

One night the battle was unusually intense. The North Koreans were firmly dug into the rock. Their positions gave them a home-court advantage against the Allied troops. They kept the night skies lighted with flares and the air crowded with bullets.

One American soldier worked his way through the maze of enemy emplacements, only to be struck down about fifty meters beyond the enemy's outer lines. Out in the darkness he screamed in pain, begging for someone to rescue him. Nobody moved. It was attempted murder for him to expect someone to help, and anyone going to his rescue would be committing suicide.

His moans and cries for help continued—unheeded.

One young man, crouched in a foxhole, kept his head down but kept lifting his wrist up into the light given off by the flares. A new flare went off, his wrist went up, and then suddenly he bolted from the safety of his foxhole to the voice crying out in the midst of the battle. Slithering and crawling, he followed the screams until he found his wounded comrade. He hoisted the wounded soldier over his shoulder and sprinted back through the enemy lines and fire to the safety of an American foxhole.

His sergeant came crawling in to find out what gave him the sudden urge for heroics. "What in the world got into you?" he asked. "Why did you take that risk?"

"It wasn't really a risk," the young man replied. "I kept checking my watch by the light of the flares until I saw that it was safe. You see, Sarge, I left on the hour because I knew that it was 9:00 a.m. back home in Kansas. My mom told me before I left that she'd be praying for me every morning at nine o'clock. I knew God would protect me."

Do you want to give your children rest for their spirits? Become a parent who prays for them every day. A bold, grace-based biblical leadership will hand them an inspired spiritual heritage.

The Painful Truth

Now for the hard part.

As I conclude this chapter, I'm reluctant to share a conviction that I have about all of this. I'm reluctant because I know that too many parents don't want to hear what I'm about to say. Because they don't want to hear it, they begin the process of rationalization, by finding fault with the person making the bold and convicting statements.

I'm going to state my conviction anyway. I'm not doing this because I'm brave. Frankly, the reactions some people have to this conviction intimidate the heck out of me. I'm not into martyrdom. I'm saying it because the battle for the hearts of our children is being lost on a grand scale, and we can't afford to allow this to happen.

Here it goes.

The type of parenting I've outlined is not idealistic. Nor is it unrealistic. It's the *bottom line.* To do it right takes *years* of concentrated *time* and *attention.*

Dads, if we think we can be effective fathers while at the same time spending fifty to sixty hours a week climbing the ladder of success, we're kidding ourselves. If we think we can dump the responsibility of raising our children off on our wives, youth group leaders, and the folks down at our local Christian school while we hide behind the breadwinner mask, we're hallucinating. Being an effective father requires personal involvement, deliberate leadership, and a strong spiritual example. We cannot—we dare not—delegate our parenting responsibilities to someone else and feel that we have fulfilled our calling to our children. It just doesn't work.

Moms, the painful truth for you is that producing secure, confident children takes a lot of hands-on attention. No one is better equipped to mother your children than you. The issue of working outside the home glares in the face of the twenty-first-century mother. Some have no choice— you're divorced, you're widowed, or your husband is unemployed. Perhaps you'd like to be home, but you can't. Most working moms, however, aren't making their decision from that position. Millions of parents have figured out how to organize their lives in the best interests of their children without requiring both parents to be gone the lion's share of each working day. Not only have so many succeeded at this, but they've also demonstrated that they can still get ahead financially, sometimes way ahead.

Work, with its ego benefits and extra income, must be weighed against the long-term needs of our children. When it comes to this issue, there are no easy answers. Loving takes time, and time requires sacrifice—somewhere. It gets painful when the sacrifices cut into our lifestyle. The lifestyle sacrifices don't have to be forever, but they may have to be for now.

Effective parenting cannot be done by accident.

We have to parent on purpose.

Those couples that are willing to swim against the current tide of cultural pressures will have a reward waiting for them. They may not be able to dress as well, drive as nice a car, go out to eat as much, or have as nice a house as those who go with the contemporary flow. But they will have the blessing of knowing they gave their kids what their kids needed most—*their parents' attention.*

When we stand before God someday, we'll have to give an account. We may have chosen, as moms and dads, to let someone else do the bulk of the heavy lifting and values programming for our kids. But it is we who will have to give an account for our children.

You may want to throw down the book at this point and forget everything we've discussed. I hope you don't. Give it some time to work in your heart. Think about it; pray about it.

Give your kids their best chance at a hopeful and fulfilling future.

MAINTAINING REST
IN THE WORK ARENA

While speaking at a conference in Texas, I met a man whose life served as a universal illustration of the frustration of maintaining rest while maintaining a career. He started talking to me while we were standing in a crowd just outside the conference center. By the way he kept strolling away from the group, I could tell he wanted a private conversation.

There was a dock overlooking a lake about a hundred feet away, so I grabbed a couple of lawn chairs and set them up just out of hearing distance toward the end of the dock. He sat for a few minutes, small-talking about his family, before he moved to the issue on his heart.

He was in sales; the job came to him naturally. He had been with his company several years and had enjoyed an admirable track record and a lucrative income. But he had hit a slump.

"Aren't slumps part of the territory?" I asked him.

He agreed. But this slump had shown him something. It had uncovered the nature of the system in which he found himself caught up.

He explained how his sales office operated. There was an executive office with paneled walls, plush carpet, nice paintings, and a beautiful desk. A metal sleeve was screwed on the door so the occupant of this office could slide in his or her nameplate. Along with it came the use of a personal secretary to help with appointments and correspondence. This was the royal treatment the Sales Leader of the Month enjoyed. This office had been his home most of the months he'd worked for his company. His million-dollar-sales plaques seldom had to be taken off the wall to make way for a new leader.

The rest of the office was an open area with cubicles and phones. The other salespeople made their appointments from these desks and shared a secretarial pool.

Over in the corner, near the door where workers passed in and out of the room, was a card table. It was for the salesperson with the poorest sales record each month. It had a pay phone hanging on the wall next to it.

This had been his "office" for the past three months.

He had a lot of financial responsibilities. He was working harder than ever, but things simply weren't happening for him. His wife was patient but worried. His kids were understanding but neglected. His boss was encouraging but getting desperate. Anyone who occupied the Loser of the Month desk for four months was automatically terminated. Company policy.

Even with this hanging over his head, he had chosen to stick with his vacation plans and take his family to their annual week of family camp. But he was finding it impossible to concentrate on the speakers or enjoy the activities with his family because he knew he might return to work the following Monday to find his awards and plaques sitting in a cardboard box next to the exit.

I asked him about the alternatives. Like getting another job. He said he could but didn't feel that it would change the bigger problem.

The bigger problem was *success:* he wanted it, he needed it, but he was tired of the demands it made on him and his family.

In his line of work, success was tangible. You could count it, look at it, live in it, polish it, drive it, wear it, and play with it. Without meaning to, he had fallen victim to a system that measures a person's value in accomplishments. He couldn't fault the system for using accomplishments as a measuring stick for rewards. But when he allowed himself to step over the line and use accomplishments as a yardstick for measuring his own value, he got caught in the trap.

The trap is the "success fantasy"—the arbitrary but deliberate standard the business world uses to motivate and control people. The man sitting at the edge of a dock in Texas was living the same nightmare experienced by men and women all over the country. He was shell-shocked from salvos the system fires at you when you're in a slump and yet was equally fatigued when he was "leading the charge."

Advising him to find another line of work wouldn't solve the bigger problem. He could become a landscaper or a painter, but the environment would still use the same yardstick for measuring a person's value. Whether you're a teacher, technician, construction worker, preacher, doctor, lawyer, or tribal chief, your job offers a hand-polished desk in a private office or a card table with a pay phone. These things might not be physical in your line of work, but they are no less real.

A former leading NBC correspondent was addressing a luncheon of businesspeople. During his career with NBC, he had enjoyed the luxury of working out of the Washington DC bureau, in touch with some of the most significant news stories of the century. Almost daily he found himself walking down the corridors of power. He candidly described the emotions that went through his mind when he found out he'd been fired. One day he had a White House press pass and could walk into the briefing room any time he wanted, and the very next day he was in the unemployment office sitting next to a truck driver with mud on his boots.

Though the unemployed truck driver had always been his equal, the journalist had worked in an arena that led him to believe he was superior. When he took his turn working at the metaphorical card table and pay phone, it cut him up inside. But it also showed him how insecure life in the paneled office can be.

Work and the money we receive from it are among the greatest contributors to restless and hurried lifestyles. They are also the hardest ones to bring under control. They go hand in hand. How we view one will determine how we handle the other.

It's easy to feel like a hostage when it comes to these two areas of your life. Even people with the best intentions find themselves in a struggle. Money and work are necessities, but they make selfish demands and don't have much concern for our needs. We can find ourselves at their mercy in an instant.

I'm like you. I want to take adequate care of my family. I'd like to engage in meaningful work. I'd like to be able to dream some big dreams and accomplish some great goals for my family. There's nothing wrong with these things. But I live in a culture that wants to program my dreams and manipulate my goals. The world in which I earn a living doesn't always share my convictions as a husband and father, and it has a bad habit of withholding rewards from people who maintain biblical attitudes toward money.

When it comes to money and work, the average family feels handcuffed to priorities that have no regard for their inner need for calm and confidence. Anxiety hits people as they dress for work on Monday morning. It jumps out at them when they total their monthly bills and see that the bank balances in Quicken aren't as big as their total deficits. They are either anxious because they're struggling to get ahead or anxious because they're trying to keep from falling behind. They are seldom granted the luxury of enjoying a position somewhere in between these two nerve-racking extremes.

What Price Excellence?

Tom Peters is the coauthor of two widely read books on the subject of work. His second book, *A Passion for Excellence,* sets forth the mandates for excellence in the work arena. He's emphatic about the need for prioritizing the customer, backing up your product with thorough service, and working from the strength of integrity. He draws his discussion of excellence to a conclusion by talking about its cost.

An honest but alarming statement appears on the last page of the last chapter of the book:

> We are frequently asked if it is possible to "have it all"—a full and satisfying personal life and a full and satisfying, hard-working professional one. Our answer is: No. The price of excellence is time, energy, attention, and focus, at the very same time that energy, attention, and focus could have gone toward enjoying your daughter's soccer game. Excellence is a high-cost item.[15]

As David Ogilvy observed in *Confessions of an Advertising Man,* "If you prefer to spend all your spare time growing roses or playing with your children, I like you better, but do not complain that you are not being promoted fast enough."[16]

Divorce, angry kids, and failing health are not the assumed requirements for success, but they are too often the by-products. Company presidents may talk about the importance of family. They may say they're committed to their employees' marriages and kids, but the actual posture of the top brass is seen on promotion day, awards day, or payday. A man who doesn't want to work overtime on Saturday because his son has a Little League game is made to feel guilty. If you pass up a promotion because it would be too demanding on your marriage, you are considered to lack ambition. Like it or not, being successful at work and being successful at home is a difficult fence to straddle.

The nightmare gets worse if the family embraces the same standards for measuring success in the home as those used in the work arena. It's so easy to buy into the myths that bigger is better, that significance is determined by superiority, or that security can be bought. These myths drive families to determine their value by their position on the social ladder, by the labels on their clothing, by the square footage of their home, or by the bottom line on their investments.

We do this because of the outspoken message of our culture. Our world makes it clear that successful men and women cannot accept second best. They can't put ceilings on their ambition. The fastest way to end up in last place is to say that you're satisfied with second place. With all of this bombarding of the American family, it's no wonder the average home has credit cards at their limit, an unaffordable mortgage, both spouses working, and no time to grow close to each other.

What Price Courage?

What we need to enjoy rest in our work is not success but *courage*. Success as the world understands it is out of our control and just beyond our reach. Because success is determined by shifting external standards, we may achieve it tomorrow only to find it redefined the day after. Courage, on the other hand, doesn't require plaques, promotions, or pedigree. But if it becomes an attitude we bring toward our work, it can reward us with rest, confidence, and calm.

I have a close friend whose father, Jim, didn't set out to be a success. He didn't plan on being a hero either. He turned out to be both. He did it with courage.

The world was at war. Red flags with swastikas and white flags with a red sun in the middle flapped in the breeze over lands they had no prior claim to. German soldiers were entrenched throughout Europe, and Japanese soldiers were entrenched on the islands of the South Pacific. The United States joined the other countries of the world to do something about it.

That's how Jim found himself inside amphibious landing equipment—four times. The battles to liberate the islands of the South Pacific started offshore as terrified young men climbed into the insides of these attack vessels. Some went once, and a few went twice, but seldom did anyone hit the beach four times. They usually didn't live long enough to have the privilege.

Jim joined thousands of men like him in facing a common enemy. He shared their fears and anxieties. He wanted to succeed in overcoming the enemy but knew that the outcome of the battle was not under his control. He could neither manipulate the enemy nor wield a great deal of control over his fellow Marines. But he did have control over himself.

So to the battle he brought the vital necessity for personal calm and ultimate victory. He brought courage.

General Ulysses S. Grant has been credited with saying, "War is minutes of terror surrounded by weeks of boredom." It takes courage to respond during the minutes of terror, but it also takes courage to remain ready during the weeks of boredom. When I think of men like Jim, I realize that they were successful because they were courageous—not courageous because they were successful. It takes courage to run into the exploding guns of the enemy, and it takes courage to keep your mind on your mission when all there is to do is sit around cleaning your weapon and counting your ammunition. A soldier's inner calm comes, therefore, not from the outcome of the battle but from his ability to maintain courage.

Calm in the workplace requires the same factor as calm on the battlefield. Those who choose to be courageous are those who are going to enjoy inner rest at their jobs. Courageous people are those who subordinate their fears to the task before them. They don't let the heat and anger of the battle distract them from their ultimate purpose.

With this in mind, let me ask a crucial question: is it possible to be a success at home and at work? I believe it is. But I believe it will only happen if we are willing to be courageous enough to make some daring decisions about our work. Men and women who take these steps of courage can enjoy confidence in the middle of the boredom and calm in the midst of battle.

Enjoying rest in the work arena requires courage in four areas. Let's examine them together.

Courage to Reject the World's View of Success

Changing the way we view success is imperative if we want to enjoy rest at work. If we go by society's view, success is determined by achievement and rewards. Self-help books and motivational speakers preach the gospel of visualization or the philosophy of "dream it today; drive it tomorrow." Success becomes a goal that is measured in status, recognition, or dollar signs. This is based on the belief that inner needs can be satisfied with things and that success is wrapped up in what you gain. If you accept this line of thinking, you will *absolutely* be denied a sense of calm and rest in your heart. Restlessness will spill over into your marriage, your children, and your health. It will do more damage than any of your accomplishments can offset.

Our culture's view of success is measured in wealth, beauty, power, and fame. There's nothing wrong with any of these things unless we need them to feel complete. Once they become the defining factors of our significance as people, we've swallowed the lure of success hook, line, and sinker. There is probably no other way for me to state my feelings on this matter than in a bold, sweeping way. So here goes:

Success should never be pursued as a goal. If you make success your goal, you are setting yourself up for intense disappointment.

Is that strong enough? This may not be the message they're preaching at work, but it is advice that, if taken, will save you from years of restlessness. Why am I so confident about this? Because I believe the American family has been fed a lie, and American business has been victimized in the process. When success is defined in dollar signs and then encouraged to become a goal, a person's motivations go through radical and damaging transformation: Superficial *things* become the object of our affections. People become commodities to be used. Playing becomes subordinate to winning. Absolute rules become relative guidelines. And individuals end up worshiping themselves. This is the theology of the success fantasy. When success is our goal, we can never be satisfied.

That's because success was never *meant* to be a goal. It was meant to be an *outcome* of certain qualities and wise priorities. Qualities such as hard work, rendering a good service and product for a fair price, backing up your work, and maintaining integrity all the way—these are the things that bring success. These qualities allow room for us to be human. To be as good as we can…but maybe not as good as the next guy. People who work hard and fair can accept their shortcomings and inevitable failures—because success for them is an outcome, not a goal. It's a process, not a product.

It's what you are, not what you do.

I ran across an excellent article by Eugene Peterson that redefines success by looking at two key players from the New Testament.

Among the apostles, the one absolutely stunning success was Judas, while the one thoroughly groveling failure was Peter. Judas was a success in the ways that most impress us: he was successful both financially and politically; he cleverly arranged to control the money of the apostolic band; and he skillfully manipulated the political forces of the day to accomplish his goals. Meanwhile, Peter was a failure in the ways we dread most: he was impotent in a crisis and socially inept; at the arrest of Jesus he collapsed, a hapless, blustering coward; in the most critical situations of his life with Jesus—the confession on the road to Caesarea Philippi and the Transfiguration on the mountain—he said the most embarrassingly inappropriate things. He wasn't the kind of companion you'd want with you in times of danger, and he wasn't the kind of person you'd feel comfortable with at a social occasion.

Time, of course, has utterly reversed our judgments on the two men. *Judas* is now a byword for *betrayal,* and Peter is one of the most honored names in the church. Judas is a villain; Peter is a saint. Yet the world continues to chase after the successes of Judas—financial wealth and political power—and defend itself against the failures of Peter—impotence and ineptness.[17]

If Peter had been employed at the same company as my frustrated friend in Texas, he would've spent a lot of time working at the card table and making appointments from the pay phone. But he still would've been one of the greatest success stories in the office.

That's because success is really the measure of your impact as a valued member of God's family. It's the essence of your significance. Real success is knowing that your value comes from God and doesn't need achievement or rewards in order to be realized. Knowing that God loved you enough to save you, forgive you, and guarantee your eternal destiny gives you the significance to be a success. It frees you up to use work as a vehicle to facilitate your family rather than as a force that holds them hostage.

Let's stop a minute and perform a mental inventory. How do you define success? Are you deriving your sense of worth and value from your accomplishments at work? Do you gauge the level of your success as a person by the lifestyle you enjoy? Could you be content even if you knew that you could never move beyond your present status at work?

I have a hard time being objective in answering these questions on my own. Maybe it would help if you asked your spouse or your children how *they* think you should answer.

We need to be courageous enough to disagree with the world's view of success. We might take some criticism. We might not advance as quickly. But we can maintain rest in the middle of a work arena intoxicated with getting ahead.

For a deeper look into this issue of the lure-of-success fantasy, especially as it pertains to grooming your children to live powerful and significant lives as adults, you might want to look at my book *Raising Kids for True Greatness.*

Courage to Accept a Level of Satisfaction

A common thread that runs through the lives of people who enjoy rest in the marketplace is the ability to be satisfied with their current lifestyle. This takes even more courage than changing one's view of success, as it runs directly counter to everything the world teaches.

Most people's income increases as they get older. Cost of living and inflation may make the net increase a minus, but the wage or salary usually goes up. There is nothing wrong with raising your standard of living as your income goes up, but somewhere along the way it's vital to reach a level of satisfaction. Those who discipline themselves to do this find their work more fulfilling because the money that is being made can go toward other worthwhile things. It also allows you to appreciate and maintain your home and possessions because they must now serve you for a longer period of time.

It takes courage for a couple to set a standard of living as a goal and then be satisfied once they reach it. The world of consumption and indulgence would consider this foolish. But the family who wants to share the gift of rest must be able to put a lid on their wants.

I have an attorney friend who bought a piece of land in an exclusive area of his midwestern town. His plans were to build on it once his ship came in. After winning a couple of landmark cases, his ship came in, docked, and was ready to be unloaded. I saw him a few months after he had received the fees for his work. I asked if he had started construction on his house.

I was impressed with his answer. He told me that he and his wife had decided their current neighborhood was a good place to live. Their children's friends were there, and the kids were enjoying their schools. They'd decided to add on to their present house and make it their long-term home. He was excited because it left them abundant resources to financially come alongside worthy endeavors and also to share with people who weren't as fortunate.

There seems to be a direct relationship between a person's heart and his checkbook. When a husband and wife decide to settle for a certain standard and stop chasing the Joneses all over town, they experience a rest in their work and in their home that no higher standard of living could supply.

It takes courage to make the choice to be satisfied.

It takes courage to invest the excess in others when you could be indulging yourself.

It takes courage to say no to wants that would only complicate your life.

But the reward of inner rest is worth it.

Courage to Maintain Rules of Good Stewardship

A lot of people defraud themselves of rest at work because they have refused to live within their means. They get mad at their job for not making them enough money. They find themselves studying the paper for better job prospects and going to a lot of interviews. The problem is that a higher-paying job won't solve their dilemma.

It's easy to make a joke about it: "I'm not overdrawn; I'm under-capitalized!" Either way, it's a restless nightmare. It's humiliating to always have to be looking over your shoulder for the bill collectors who are pursuing you. But debt keeps you that way. And it spoils the joy you could be receiving from work.

People who struggle to live within their means follow a similar pattern—they neglect their needs to satisfy their wants:

- They have a new car but are behind on the rent.
- They can't afford to take their baby in for a checkup but can afford cable TV.
- They can't afford braces for their kids' teeth but can afford to go to the lake regularly to play with their boat.
- They can't afford to save but eat out regularly and occasionally stop by the casino on the way home.

It takes courage to admit that you may be holding your family hostage because of poor stewardship. It takes courage to get out of debt. It takes courage to *stay* out of debt. But those who are willing to face this issue and do something about it are in the best position to bring rest to their work lives.

It doesn't matter whether we live on a fixed income or an open-ended bonus, a wage or a draw, all families are better off on a budget. And the more you make, the more you should live on a budget. Jesus weighed in on this issue: "When someone has been entrusted with much, even more will be required" (Luke 12:48, NLT). In other words, the more we make and the more we have, the more accountable we are to God for how we handle it. That's why budgets are non-negotiable for calm and rested families. A good budget provides for payment of bills for necessities (food, clothing, shelter); investment in now (entertainment or "wants"); investment in the future (savings); and investment in eternity (giving to God's work in the world).

If you have to cut, start with the entertainment and "wants" section. Once again, that takes courage. It flies in the face of the average person's programming and desires. But those who exercise strong-minded determination in this area of their lives get to reap the reward of going to work without a gun to their head.

No statement on finding rest *in* your work would be complete without a reminder to find rest *from* your work. God's Word doesn't leave this principle open for debate. The Bible is outspoken on the subject of taking a day off. God established it as a pattern when He created the earth:

Thus the heavens and the earth were completed, and all their hosts. By the seventh day God completed His work which He had done, and He rested on the seventh day from all His work which He had done. Then God blessed the seventh day and sanctified it, because in it He rested from all His work which God had created and made. (Genesis 2:1–3, NASB)

After God established the pattern, He established the principle of the Sabbath:

Remember the sabbath day, to keep it holy. Six days you shall labor and do all your work, but the seventh day is a sabbath of the LORD your God; in it you shall not do any work.... For in six days the LORD made the heavens and the earth, the sea and all that is in them, and rested on the seventh day; therefore the LORD blessed the sabbath day and made it holy. (Exodus 20:8–11, NASB)

Workaholism may be applauded by the corporate structure and may provide the surest route to the top, but God says it's wrong. He wants us to observe a day off. Our brain needs it, our body needs it, our spirit needs it, and our family needs it. It's a commandment designed to make us more effective and useful to the people we are called to serve.

Courage to Sacrifice the Now for the Forever

The man I spoke of at the opening of this chapter wanted solutions to his frustration. He didn't want to continue working from the card table in the corner, but he wasn't sure that he or his family would weather the pressure that went with the key to the Salesman of the Month's office either. He was about to overdose on Tums because of the stress.

The answer for him is the answer for a lot of people: he had to muster up the courage to sacrifice. What he ended up having to do was sacrifice his standard of living. He and his wife decided that, while being in last place wasn't acceptable, being in first place simply carried too high a price tag. The demands that first place required were directly at the expense of the time needed by his children. So he chose a path that gave him an adequate income, though not as much as he was used to. By cutting out some of the extras in his life, he learned a good lesson about contentment. He learned that his family was actually happier and closer having less than they were with having all the amenities the pressure provided. In the long run, his greater contentment made him much more valuable to the marketplace. A couple years after he made the adjustments, he was making far more than he'd ever made in the middle of the rat race but with far more balance in his overall schedule.

I love stories with happy endings, don't you?

Is there a happy ending for your story too?

It all depends on your choices. You may need the courage to sacrifice in order to bring a sense of rest and contentment back into your job. People prepared to make hard decisions stand to win the most in life.

You may not be qualified for your job. Pray for the courage to admit it.

You may not be trained for your job. Develop a strategy to get the help you need.

You may not make enough money. Be prepared to cut your spending until you can get a raise or a higher-paying job.

You may not be conscientious at your job. Have the courage to confess it as a sin against God, yourself, your family, and your employer.

You may not like your job. Endure it with a good attitude as a necessity for the income of your family until you can get something better.

We all need the courage to be honest with ourselves about our work. We need to keep in mind that it is a vehicle to accommodate the people we love. It is an opportunity to make a contribution and receive fair compensation. But if it becomes a consuming god that we worship or a dreaded nuisance that we neglect, it will drain us of the rest it could offer. Work is a privilege and a responsibility. It's not that you have to work but that you get to.

Charles Kingsley put it this way:

Thank God every morning when you get up that you have something to do which must be done, whether you like it or not. Being forced to work, and forced to do your best, will breed in you temperance and self-control, diligence and strength of will, cheerfulness and contentment, and a hundred virtues which the idle never know.[18]

GAINING REST IN YOUR RELATIONSHIPS

My town's nickname is "The Valley of the Sun." Phoenix is an oasis in the middle of the arid Arizona desert. The mountains that rise up out of the desert floor present a stark and haunting beauty to the skyline. They also present a temptation.

There is something about a mountain that brings out the ego in people. We see it and we just have to conquer it. It has something to do with it "being there." Mountains are nature's giants, its Goliaths. And men and women get this strange craving to dominate them.

For those who want to do it the easy way (like me), the mountains have well-kept paths with rest stops along the way. But there are always the daring and adventurous who want to make their own path. They study the mountain and try to figure out the worst way to go from the bottom to the top, and then they take off.

I've learned something about the mountains in our valley: they're not very merciful. They have a special way of showing their temper with those people who choose to challenge their more treacherous surfaces.

The cacti, scorpions, and rattlesnakes are the lesser of the obstacles. The greatest threat is the mountain itself.

Camelback Mountain lies on the east side of our valley, its silhouette true to its name. This gigantic "sleeping camel" looks appropriate resting in the middle of the desert. But even though it appears to be sleeping, it holds a lot of lively surprises for climbers thinking they can just slip up its back.

Creased behind the right "ear" of Camelback Mountain is Echo Canyon. It is a deep cutaway that tempts a lot of hikers and mountain climbers. Its cliffs are difficult for them to pass up.

One of the rare times I was in this canyon, an accident occurred. A climber had tried to scale the cliff and lost his footing. He dropped quite a ways before a stone tooth sticking out from the cliff caught his body. I wasn't very close to the scene of the accident, but from my vantage point I could see a small group of people leaning out over a ledge and looking down. Their animated movements made it obvious that someone had fallen.

Search-and-rescue people were summoned, and Air Evac waited in the wings. It took a while for the experienced team of rescuers to arrive. It took even longer for them to get what they came for.

Because of where the climber had fallen and the extent of his injuries, it was impossible to simply lower someone down on the end of a rope and bring him up. There was no way for the helicopter to descend close enough to the cliffs to empty out a team on the precipice that held the victim.

I watched from a distance through binoculars as men spoke into their walkie-talkies. I don't know who they were talking to, but in about ten minutes a helicopter came up from the other side of the mountain and hovered over them. It lowered its package in a few seconds and then flew away. The men tore open the package and started assembling something from the materials inside.

From the look of it, they had done this before. In a few brief minutes, a rescue platform was hovering over the side of the cliff. Cables had been nailed into the rock, and the tiny scaffolding beneath it had been anchored.

Within seconds after the platform had been secured, men were rappelling off its side. A rescue basket followed them down from cables hooked to the edge. The men disappeared briefly. I knew they had the fallen climber when the men still on the platform started cranking up the basket. By the time the basket cleared the edge of the cliff, Air Evac was hovering over top. They hoisted the fallen man onto the platform and in the same motion connected him to the hook that had been lowered from the helicopter. About ten seconds later this injured climber was inside the airborne ambulance, racing to the nearest emergency room.

A fallen climber. It sounds like a contradiction. In reality, the two words go together—they are inseparable. Every climber who starts up the side of a mountain realizes that falling is a possibility. He may fear the inevitable fall and do everything in his power to avoid it, but he can't eliminate the possibility of it if he is committed to the climb.

Scaling the Future

As the clock pulls the future closer, we realize that it is going to be an era of challenge and change like nothing we have ever experienced. This new century looms before us like a great mountain, and we've only just begun to climb. The future is overwhelming and threatening to those who don't like challenges. We are climbing in the context of an international war on terror. Political instability is a cliché on every continent. And the explosion of information and technology is making a lot of the training we received just last year obsolete. These factors can be extremely intimidating to those who don't look forward to change.

A lot of people have reason to be threatened by the presence of something as massive and mysterious as the future. We'd like to live life one day at a time, but the sophistication of this information age won't allow it. Like it or not, the future is a force to be reckoned with, and those who want to take it one day at a time are probably going to have the most problems with it.

That's because the future, like the mountains that surround my home, isn't going to be very merciful to inexperienced, casual climbers. It's going to be tough enough on those who know what they're doing. This is the very nature of change. Changing times are surprising times, and one thing that people climbing mountains don't want are surprises.

We won't be able to go around the future. We may desire to stay camped at its base, stuck in the past. But that probably won't work. We've learned from history that those who fight progress seldom win. Progress has a way of bulldozing over those who want to hang on to yesterday.

Like it or not, the future is coming. The best way to deal with it is to plan on making the climb.

Personally, that thought gets me very excited. I don't want to stay camped in the past. The future might represent challenge and change, but it also holds many great opportunities. The vistas we will see as we climb to the top of the future are going to offer us more perspective than we've ever had before. The mountain of the future is filled with secrets, but they will become our new discoveries. Those discoveries are going to bring new challenges and opportunities for the resourceful and industrious people who embrace them.

But good and bad follow each other around. The future will also offer new threats to the family, new competition for marriages, and new anxiety for the restless spirit of human beings. That's why we can't plan on scaling it alone.

You Have a Friend

If we want to make it through the future in one piece, we're going to need some help. The pressures of change are going to make it more difficult to solo. Families will have to team up—and be closer than ever before. But we're going to need more than that. We'll need a network of people surrounding us and helping us as we make our way. This network of support so vital for the future is the same network we need so desperately in the present. If we ever expect to negotiate the treacherous climb of the future, we are going to have to establish a strong climbing team now.

Two groups make up this team—friends and the church. Both are necessary. The family that has friends and a church is the family that doesn't need to fear what is coming.

Friends and the church satisfy two crucial needs in our lives. First of all, they provide *support*. They are helping hands and strong arms that help pull us over the rough spots. They are the ones who serve as our search-and-rescue team when we fall. They join us in celebrating our victories and share tears with us in our sorrows.

The second crucial need that friends and church satisfy is *accountability*. These people help keep us on the path. They become the caution signs and guardrails that keep us out of danger. Support and accountability are crucial needs for the family pressured by the demands of life.

When I was watching the search-and-rescue team recover the man who had fallen off Camelback Mountain, I was impressed by how well they knew their job. But even these professionals needed equipment and resources to perform their task. The helicopters, the strong platform, and the professional-grade climbing equipment set them free to do their work thoroughly and effectively.

We need friends, but we also need the equipment to help us when we're down. The church provides that well-anchored rescue platform, the ropes, and the safety harnesses. It is that visible structure, anchored on the Rock that cannot be shaken.

But what if the equipment hasn't been maintained? What if the cables are defective and the steel rods of the platform weak? What if the ropes are rotting and frayed? What if the rescuers don't know what they're doing? Because amateurs can masquerade as professionals and faulty equipment can look good on the surface, we need to be careful. Friends will occasionally be called on to help us through tough times. We have to make sure we have tough friends. And a church can look great on the outside, but can it serve as the platform of strength and provide the barriers of protection we so desperately need?

If we want to maintain rest as we scale the mountain peaks of change and uncertainty, we need competent friends and a responsible church. These aren't impossible to find. We just need to know what we're looking for.

The Profile of a Good Friend

Friendships are maintained at different levels of commitment. They run the gamut from casual, fair-weather friends to loving, intimate friends. Most people have a large group of friends who fall into the first category and only a handful (maybe only one) who fall into the second category. When you lose your footing or get lost in your climb through the crags and cliffs of life, it doesn't matter how many casual friends you have. It only matters that you have someone you would consider a true and loving friend.

Loving friends are the people who come to your mind when you're confused and need advice, when you're worried and in need, when you receive good news and just have to tell someone. They are the first ones on your guest list, the first choice for an evening out. They're the ones you would trust with your possessions, your kids, your life. Their job is a big one. Over the course of a lifetime they must serve as confidant, counselor, referee, prophet, and pallbearer.

If you can claim only one such friend in your lifetime, consider yourself rich.

Because they play such a key part in our lives, we must choose these close friends carefully and cultivate them regularly. But not knowing what to look for in a friend sends a lot of people off course in their search. We can easily become sidetracked when we look for characteristics like compatibility, common interests, and personality. These things are important, but they're not the kind of characteristics that can help us through our hurts.

If I'm going to be taking risks as I climb the mountains that rise up out of my circumstances and experiences, I want a couple of people around me who exhibit three characteristics. My observation is that those who have these three qualities can be your greatest source of genuine rest besides God and your family.

Loyalty

None of us wants to be put on hold when we call on our friends. We need to know they'll be there when we need them.

Loyal friends assume the best about us. They defend us when we are accused. They stand by our side when we are guilty and help us endure our shame. This doesn't mean that they wink at our sin or trivialize the severity of our mistakes. But their loyalty keeps them close to us even when we have to walk through the dark valleys of our own regrets.

One of my closest friends is a man named Kory. We've enjoyed a lot of laughs and discussed a lot of hurts. I've always felt that Kory would never desert me in times of trouble. That's because he understands loyalty. If I did something horrible—shamed my family and my reputation—most people would turn away from me. I've always felt, however, that Kory's the kind of guy who would never turn his back on me. If I ever went to prison, he would visit me.

I'm fortunate to have several friends like Kory. They are loyal in good times and bad. For obvious reasons, I don't plan to put their loyalty to the test. But it's nice to know they have this quality if I ever need it.

Honesty

Good friends must be honest. It's an extremely rare quality in a friend. It's hard to find because we don't encourage our friends to exercise it in our lives. But if I want to make it through the climb, I need friends who will be straightforward, candid, and sincere.

Proverbs 27:6 is one of those verses you wish wasn't in the Bible but are glad is after you've felt its strength. It says, "Faithful are the wounds of a friend, but deceitful are the kisses of an enemy" (NASB).

Accountability is painful. There comes a time in all of our lives when we need to hear the truth that hurts. None of us likes to be confronted when we're wrong, but fortunate is the man or woman who has a friend who loves enough to risk rejection and tell the truth anyway.

We need to encourage the people close to us to not be timid about pointing out danger areas during our climb. And we don't need to get defensive if they point out our poor climbing techniques. A friend's honesty can save us a lot of pain.

Sensitivity

A third quality of a good friend is a genuine sensitivity to our needs and feelings. Friends need to recognize that our feelings, our secrets, and our hopes are treasures that must be guarded.

A sensitive person knows when a joke has gone too far. He has a way of recognizing when our frustrations are hitting the kindling point. He gets good at knowing when to get close and when to give us room. His caution with privileged information assures us that our secrets are safe with him.

Very few people get straight A's on their friendship report card. On the subjects of loyalty, honesty, and sensitivity, the best friend you have may only maintain a C average. Don't panic. Good friendships don't just happen. They are deliberately planned and developed over a lifetime.

The best way to get good friends is to be one. People who develop the qualities of loyalty, honesty, and sensitivity in their lives stand a better chance of attracting friends who have these qualities too.

The best mountain climbers in the world seek each other out. If they're going to take on the biggest challenges, they want to do it with the best team. Whether we are scaling the cliffs that surround us in the present or the mountains of change that loom in the future, we need good friends on our climbing team. They will help keep our hearts at rest when our lives are dangling over the edge.

The Profile of a Good Church

If we must climb our way through today and over tomorrow, we need more than a few friends. We need competent coaching, accurate maps, and reliable equipment. Going forward in life requires us to face myriad unknowns. The church can help provide what we need to face these unknowns.

The church is an extended family. It is an organism made up of a lot of families with common goals. But a pretty building and a steeple do not mean that a church is equipped to equip. Churches are like people—some know what they're doing and some don't. Choosing a good church is crucial.

There are no perfect churches, just as there are no perfect friends and no perfect people. Any time people are involved, there are going to be problems. Churches are families, and all families suffer from certain degrees of dysfunction. But there are criteria that I believe can be used as a yardstick, and a good church—even with its problems—should be able to measure up in each area.

For our discussion, let's call these criteria the focus points of the church. Although I won't list all that I consider important, these three will give you the best chance of finding a church that can help you maintain rest in your soul.

A Focus on the Lord

This point, you may think, should go without saying. Unfortunately, many churches with a cross on the roof and Christ in a stained-glass window in fact have little to do with either. That's because God's Spirit has no influence on them. These types of churches are more like religious country clubs—they meet people's social and physical needs, but they don't meet their spiritual needs.

My conviction is that a church cannot equip us for the climb if it cannot bring us to God. I also maintain the conviction that if a church wants to bring us to God, it must ultimately take us down a path that leads to the foot of the cross. In other words, it isn't God in general but Jesus in particular that we need.

Before we place our family under the authority of a church, we must be certain that the church is under the authority of God. Listen closely to the sermon next Sunday. It won't be hard to determine if your church is focused on the Lord.

A Focus on the Scriptures

A church that can deliver rest to a human heart must speak and operate from the authority of Scripture. God didn't leave us in the dark; He gave clear instructions.

The end of the twentieth century and the dawn of the twenty-first has been a difficult time for the church. People who have only been around a few decades have concluded that the Bible, which has been around for a few millennia, isn't relevant today. Many of these people stand in ornate pulpits throughout our country. The Bible is not the subject of their sermons but often the object of their ridicule.

When I deal with people who go to churches that do not respect the Word of God, I pick up an insecurity in them that runs deep. They are starving for rest because they have been denied truth. When we go to church, we don't want sermons and teaching based strictly on human opinions. We need the truth that jumps from every page of the Bible.

A church that facilitates rest, then, is a church that focuses on the Lord Jesus and focuses on His truth.

A Focus on the Family

Churches committed to helping us on our climb through the canyons of time must have a focus on the parent/child dynamic that makes up the foundation of our culture. As parents, we need all the help we can get. Our children need instruction that reinforces our values.

A church committed to the family recognizes its responsibility. It must be an ally to the parent and an asset to the home. It must recognize its calling to bring order and calm to a confusing world. It must do more than give lip service to the priority of healthy families by creating ongoing training and support for marriages, parents, and grandparents that empower family members to carry the bulk of the responsibility for healthy spiritual relationships within the home. That's because, when you bottom-line this whole discussion, strong churches don't make strong families; strong families make strong churches.

Good churches enfold the hurting and the helpless. They are a haven for the hurried and a guiding light to the confused. They offer their love to the outcast, their encouragement to the fearful parent, and their sensitive rebuke to those who are walking too close to the sheer cliffs and dangerous drop-offs of twenty-first-century culture.

Sundays can be the highlight of a family's week if that family has the privilege of being part of a church with its priorities properly aligned. Restless hearts need the church. Outside of our immediate family, the church is the only organization that will commit to seeing us into the world, helping us through life, and standing by our side as we slip into the beyond.

A Focus on Grace

Families that want to enjoy the rewards of calm and peace in the middle of their hurried lives need to be attending churches that focus on the Lord, His Word, and families. But there is one factor that determines if any of these focuses have lasting impact. That factor is a church's ability to function in the power of God's amazing grace.

Many churches understand what grace looks like when it comes to gaining forgiveness from sins and eternal life through Christ. What they have a difficult time figuring out is what grace looks like in the *ongoing* relationship with Christ. The sad truth is that many churches offer grace when it comes to salvation but grief when it comes to living our day-to-day lives. The Christian's life is distilled down to a checklist of arbitrary dos and don'ts that we perform in order to curry God's continued favor.

Here's the problem with that. We don't have to do anything to curry God's favor; we already have it! His love, mercy, and grace aren't carrots He holds out in front of us. They are part of the basic DNA of His relationship with us. Obviously, a good church will teach the non-negotiable truths of God's Word, but it doesn't extract obedience through the toxic power of shame, guilt, or self-righteous expectations. Families that want to enjoy the upside benefit of a grace-based relationship with Christ need to worship in a church that motivates them to love and good deeds by encouraging them to a deeper, passionate, and courageous confidence in the overwhelming power and presence of God in their lives.

Churches that bring the best out of people are churches that deal with the members of their congregations the same way God deals with His family. God knows our deepest longings, He sees our truest needs, He understands our greatest challenges, He envisions our highest potential. These are qualities of God's grace that take the tension out of our days and the anxiety out of our relationships. Grace-based churches exude these very same qualities.

Climb Every Mountain

It's possible to maintain a calm and confident heart as we climb the mountains ahead. The right friends and the right path are all that we need. We can anticipate a few surprises; we can count on a few stumbles; we may even find that falling over the edge a time or two is unavoidable. But the right people with the right rescue equipment can make it all bearable.

We need not fear the mountains of change. They are ours to climb. From their pinnacles we will gain a new perspective on the life God has called us to live.

Epilogue

ROAD SIGNS

In the early 1980s, the air-traffic controllers' union and the White House decided to play a game of chicken. I was one of the millions of airline travelers who found themselves in the middle of the game. The tickets for my trips only served to prove that, at one time, I'd had a reserved seat on a scheduled flight. Flights were being canceled by the minute. The only laws that were still in force were the laws of aerodynamics, but it was hard to find a plane on which you could actually enjoy them.

That's what caused me to arrive late at a Michigan airport. The pastor picking me up was a warm, sensitive man, but he didn't rate high on flexibility. A large group of teenagers was assembling at a camp in central Michigan, and I was supposed to be there with them at that very moment.

That's how I found myself rocketing up the interstate in a subcompact, moving considerably faster than a respectable preacher's car ought to travel. We headed north on a freeway that cuts up the middle of the state, the immediate countryside little more than a green blur out my window. Gripped by hurry and worry, my driver bent over the wheel with set jaw and clenched teeth. My own relaxed demeanor probably infuriated him. But why get excited? I'd long since learned that when you're working with teenagers, the schedule should be written in pencil.

My companion, however, still viewed the program as some immutably perfect plan. He couldn't imagine such a thing as adapting to changes imposed on us by outside forces. As he drove and worried, I sat back to enjoy the ride and maybe get some rest. The problem was, he wouldn't slow down. When we passed a Porsche, I started to get nervous.

Then something caught my eye in the distance as we screamed north along the freeway. Even at that speed, you couldn't miss it. It was so tall and distinct you could see it from more than a mile away.

It was a cross.

I've seen bold statements about the Christian faith placed in strategically visible locations before. The people who put them there have good intentions, but most of them come off as too imposing for my evangelistic tastes. But being a Christian, I naturally wanted to read the message printed across the horizontal beam of the cross. As we passed by, I saw that the message was not for evangelistic purposes as much as it was to direct people to an out-of-the-way attraction.

The message read: "See Where the Hymn 'Old Rugged Cross' Was Written." The narrow road that stretched off into the country looked lonely and untraveled. I asked my worried driver about the sign. He remarked that he had seen the sign before but had never bothered to see where it led. But we had people waiting and messages to communicate, so we hastened on.

A couple of exits farther north, we pulled off the highway and drifted through a small town. Just about a mile or so along, we came to the conference center where I would be speaking all week. The kids were having a great time. They seemed oblivious to the fact that circumstances weren't cooperating with "the plan."

We assembled them in the chapel, the program began, I spoke, and my ministerial chauffeur began to relax. I even caught him smiling. By the next morning, summer camp was back on schedule.

As I was going through the motions of my responsibilities as camp pastor, I found my mind slipping down the freeway a few exits. *See Where the Hymn "Old Rugged Cross" Was Written.* Maybe it was my interest in the past or my natural curiosity for out-of-the-way corners of life, but I felt that I couldn't afford to be this close and not go the extra mile to see what this message on the freeway was all about.

After morning chapel on Thursday, I grabbed a hymn book and obtained permission from the camp manager to borrow a camp vehicle. In about ten minutes I was heading out on the dirt road in search of the cross.

If you've ever worked with camps, then you know that camp vehicles seldom meet the dictionary definition of transportation. I was in a pickup truck. It wasn't very old, but it was already a piece of junk. It had been given to the camp recently. I had a feeling that the best miles had been driven out of it by some member of a church, and then it was "donated to the Lord's service" at the point when the value of the tax deduction was greater than the value of the trade-in. It felt like it was held together by wire and duct tape, and it steered like a sled. The radio had a bad connection, so I decided I'd have to miss the opportunity to listen to the local country station.

Instead, I hummed the tune to the song whose title had been painted on that distinct sign that had caught my attention. In less than an instant, I found myself heart-deep in nostalgia.

You know how it is. You hear a song you haven't heard for a long time, and something sends the circuits in your brain sifting through the seldom-used files of your memory. Certain songs mysteriously attach themselves to places or people in your past. Just a few notes is all it takes to fill you with bittersweet, half-remembered emotions.

I found myself back in Pennsylvania, standing in church, sharing a hymn book with Mom and Dad, singing those redemptive words.

On a hill far away...

I knew all the words before I could read. The hymn was one of the standards, a classic that anyone who went to a Protestant church would know.

I pulled off the highway and headed east through the rolling Michigan countryside. Almost immediately I came upon a small village that looked like it hadn't changed much in fifty years. It had an anemic look to it. The buildings needed painting, the streets were dirty, and the people looked bored.

I kept following the road, expecting to see little signs leading the way. There was nothing. Just country road and countryside. After a couple of miles of wandering around, I decided to double back to the little town and see if I could get some help.

A man who looked as if he worked hard for a living was the first person I saw. I slowed down and got his attention with my question. He knew the place I was looking for and gave me a few directions.

You know how it is when you develop a mental picture of something that predetermines what you think you'll find—only to find yourself disappointed when you get there? I'd been picturing a little frame house with a few rooms and some antique furniture. I figured there'd be some photos of the songwriter and a history of his life.

All I found was a simple cross by a half-circle driveway that looped off the isolated road. The sign on the cross conveyed the message that George Bennard had lived on this site, and it was here that he wrote the hymn that would become an inspiration to millions of people for generations to come.

I climbed out of the truck and walked out onto the grass by the side of the driveway. I was standing on the top of a slight hill. It was raised just enough to provide a good look at the surrounding landscape. I walked out about a hundred feet from the truck to take in the view. When I turned around to walk back, I noticed a faint outline in the grass. The shadow of a cross fell across the lines of the old foundation upon which Mr. Bennard's house had been built.

The house was gone. Only the cross was standing.

Retrieving the hymnal from the pickup, I walked to where I figured the walls of this little house had stood. I sat down in the grass, looked up the hymn in the index, and leafed through to the appropriate page.

The editor of the hymnal indicated that Mr. Bennard had written the song in 1913. I thought to myself that life had certainly changed since he had put his poem of hope to music. We were now exploring Martian terrain, while he lived in an era when aviation was barely out of the cradle.

I was glad I had paid attention in history class, because my mind started clicking out information that made me rethink my original contrast of times. When George Bennard sat in this house composing his beautiful hymn, his world was exploding with new technology and information. Automobiles, electric lights, telephones, phonographs, and radio were already altering the way people thought. A few months after he penned his hymn, young men from all over the world would put on uniforms and meet in the trenches of Europe to fight the "war to end all wars." Some of them would come from the very towns through which I had driven that morning. The League of Nations, the United Nations, and scores of other alliances would attempt and fail to maintain the peace these men fought for. World War I would be a costly dress rehearsal for World War II and the unending conflicts that have followed it to the present day.

Mr. George Bennard was part of a generation of people who began the maddening marathon our generation is still running. He was feeling the pressure of rapid change just as we do, and he took comfort in the permanence and hope of a bloodstained cross erected almost two thousand years ago. The inspiration that helped him write his song in the first part of the twentieth century was still working in the heart of a man sitting in Bennard's backyard many decades later.

I set the open hymnal down in the grass and began to sing the words out loud:

On a hill far away stood an old rugged cross,
  The emblem of suffering and shame. [19]

Although I could never forget the first stanza to this song, I was glad I'd brought the hymnal with me. I needed those other stanzas to complete the impression of that moment on my hurried heart. I thought of George Bennard sitting at a little desk or upright piano looking out his window. A confidence in his heart allowed him to look beyond the hills of Michigan to a hill outside of Jerusalem and the cross that was built for the God-who-became-a-man.

A cross...by a freeway. It seems a fitting conclusion to our study of hurried lifestyles.

The title of this book is an intentional play on words. "Little House" reminds us of a long-ago era of tranquillity and rest. "Freeway" is a like-it-or-not statement of where we are—and a promise of where we're going.

It's the symbol of a life that moves too fast.

But we have to keep going. We can't go back. And you know, I really wouldn't want to even if I could. The future holds too many exciting possibilities, too many intriguing opportunities.

But along our high-speed journey, a simple cross calls us to pull over, to take a side trip few people seem to have time for. They have schedules and deadlines, goals and objectives. The "program" looms large, and detours don't fit the itinerary.

Those who do make the journey find lonely back roads and people who don't seem to fit the dress-for-success mentality. Sometimes they're disappointed with their initial visit. They expect to find the comfort of man-made shrines and the mementos of human accomplishments. Yet the memories of men crumble all too soon, leaving only the distinct silhouette of the timeless, ageless cross.

The signs pointing the way to the cross won't be neon-lighted and twenty feet high. If you're not watching, you could drive right by. But those who slow down long enough to negotiate the turn and make the side trip to a back road in Palestine have a promise waiting for them from the Lord of the cross:

> You will seek Me and find Me when you search for Me with all your heart. (Jeremiah 29:13, NASB)

101 WAYS TO GIVE
REST TO YOUR FAMILY

Becoming good at the things that build inner confidence and calm takes practice—and a dash of creativity! The following list might provide some cloud seeding for a brainstorm or two of your own. Have some fun with your family—and get ready for a good rest.

1. Pay off your credit cards, and keep them paid off.
2. Take off ten pounds (at least), or accept where you are without any more complaints.
3. Eat dinner together as a family at least three nights a week.
4. Men: take your wife on a dialogue date. (No movie, guys.)
5. Read your kids a classic book. Twain's a good start.
6. Memorize the Twenty-third Psalm as a family.
7. Give each family member a hug for twenty-one days in a row. (That's how long the experts say it takes to develop a habit.)
8. Pick at least three nights of the week when the television will remain off.
9. Go out for a non–fast food dinner as a family.

10. Pray for your spouse and children every day.

11. Plan a vacation together.

12. Take a vacation together.

13. Read a chapter from the Bible every day until it becomes a habit.

14. Sit together as a family in church.

15. Surprise your teenager: wash his car and fill up his gas tank.

16. Take an afternoon off work and surprise your child by excusing her from school and taking her to a ball game.

17. Take a few hours one afternoon and go to the library as a family.

18. Take a walk as a family.

19. Write each member of your family a letter sharing why you value them.

20. Give your spouse a weekend getaway with a friend to a place of his or her choice.

21. Go camping as a family.

22. Go to bed early (one hour before your normal bedtime) every day for a week.

23. Take each of your children out to breakfast (individually) four or five times a year throughout their childhood.

24. Text message your kids just to tell them that you love them.

25. Religiously wear your seat belts.

26. Get a complete physical at least every five years.

27. Exercise a little at least three days out of every week.

28. Make sure you have adequate life insurance on both you and your spouse.

29. Write out details about finances, wills, and important business information that your spouse can use to keep things under control in the event of your death.

30. Make sure your family car is safe (tires, brakes, etc.), and get it tuned up.

31. Replace the batteries in your smoke alarms.

32. Put a security system in your house.

33. Attend the parent/teacher meetings of each child as a couple. If you're divorced, bury the hatchet and present a united concern at these meetings.

34. Help your kids with their homework.

35. Dads: watch the kids on Saturday while your wife goes shopping. And if a friend calls, don't say you're "baby-sitting." You're just being a dad.

36. Have a "no Internet, e-mail, IM, or texting night" once a week.

37. Put together a picture puzzle of five hundred pieces or more as a family.

38. Take time during the week to read a Bible story to your children and then discuss it with them.

39. Encourage each child to submit to you his or her most perplexing question, and promise that you'll either answer it or discuss it.

40. Finish fixing something around the house.

41. Tell your kids how you and your spouse met.

42. Tell your kids about your first date.

43. Sit down and write your parents a letter thanking them for a specific thing they did for you. (Don't forget to send it!)

44. Spend an evening out as a family when everyone's cell phone is left at home.

45. Keep a prayer journal for a month. Keep track of the specific ways God meets your needs.

46. Do some stargazing away from the city with your family, and help your children identify constellations. Conclude the evening with prayer to the majestic God who created the heavens.

47. Men: treat your wife to a beauty makeover (massage, facial, manicure, haircut, etc.).

48. Give the little kids an alternative to watching Saturday morning cartoons (breakfast at McDonald's, garage sales, the park, chores, etc.).

49. Ask your children each day about the highlights or low points of the day at school.

50. After you make your next major family decision, take your children back through the process and teach them how you arrived at your decision.

51. Start saying to yourself, *My car doesn't look so bad.*

52. Call your spouse from work just to see how he or she is doing.

53. Compile a family tree, and teach your children the history of their ancestors.

54. Walk through an old graveyard with your children, and discuss the epitaphs.

55. Say no to at least one thing a day—even if it's only a second piece of pie.

56. The next time you see a great and redemptive show on television, write a letter to the network that broadcast the show thanking them for the investment in your family.

57. Turn off the lights and turn on some inspirational music as you focus your thoughts on the Lord.

58. Write a note to your pastor praising him for something.

59. Take back all the books in your library that actually belong in someone else's library.

60. Give irritating drivers the right to pull in front of you without signaling; don't yell at them.

61. Make every effort not to let the sun go down on your anger.

62. Accept legitimate criticism from your spouse or friend without reacting or defending yourself.

63. If your car has a Christian bumper sticker on it, drive accordingly.

64. Maintain ongoing training and development in your spiritual responsibilities as a spouse, a parent, or a grandparent.[20]

65. Make a list of people who have hurt your feelings over the past year; then check your list to see if you've forgiven them.

66. Make a decision to honor your parents, even if they made a career out of dishonoring you.

67. Dads: take your children to the dentist and doctor for your wife.

68. Play charades with your family, but limit subjects to memories from the past.

69. Men: clean up the kitchen for your wife. Women: clean up the garage for your husband.

70. Schedule yourself a free day during summer break to stay home with your family.

71. Get involved in a family project that serves or helps someone less fortunate.

72. As a family, get involved in a recreational activity.

73. Men: send your wife flowers.

74. Spend an evening going through old pictures from family vacations.

75. Take a weekend once a year for you and your spouse to get away and renew your relationship.

76. Praise your spouse and children—in their presence—to someone else.

77. Discuss a world or national problem, and ask your children for their opinion on it.

78. Wait up for your teenagers when they are out on a date.

79. Have a "quiet Sunday"—no television, no radio, no stereo, no computer, no cell phones, no iPods…no kidding.

80. If your children are little, spend an hour playing with them each week—but let *them* determine the game.

81. Have your parents tell your children about life when they were young.
82. Give up TV shows that prey on your sexual fantasies.
83. Declutter your house.
84. If you have a habit of watching late-night television but have to be at work early every morning, change your habit.
85. Don't accept unnecessary business breakfast appointments.
86. E-mail missionaries regularly.
87. Go through your closets, and give everything you haven't worn in a year to a relief organization.
88. Become a faithful and frequent visitor of your church's library.
89. Become a monthly supporter of a Third World child.
90. Keep each child's mementos, school projects, awards, etc., in a separate file. You'll appreciate these when they've left the nest.
91. Read the biography of a missionary or great Christian leader from history.
92. Give regularly and faithfully to conscientious church endeavors.
93. Place with your will a letter to each family member telling why you were glad you got to share life with him or her.
94. Go through your CDs, DVDs, and downloads, and discard any that might be a bad example to your children.
95. Furnish a corner of a room with comfortable chairs, and declare it the "disagreement corner." When a conflict arises, go to this corner and don't leave until it's resolved.
96. Give each child the freedom to pick his or her favorite dinner menu at least once a month.
97. Go over to a shut-in's house as a family, and completely clean it and get the yard work done.
98. Call an old friend from your past just to see how he or she is getting along.

99. Get a good friend to hold you accountable for a specific important need (Bible reading, prayer, spending time with your family, losing a few pounds, etc.).
100. Establish a budget and live on it.
101. Go to a Christian marriage enrichment seminar at least every other year.[21]

NOTES

1. Charles Swindoll, *Killing Giants, Pulling Thorns* (Portland, OR: Multnomah, 1978), 79.
2. Andor Foldes, "Beethoven's Kiss," *Reader's Digest* (November 1986), 145.
3. Artie Glenn, "Crying in the Chapel," copyright © 1953, Valley Publishing.
4. Rodger Strader, "There Is Peace," copyright © 1982, Belwin-Mills.
5. Isaac Watts, "At the Cross," 1707, public domain.
6. Meg Greenfield, "Why Nothing Is 'Wrong' Anymore," *Newsweek* (July 28, 1986), 72.
7. Susanna McBee, "Morality," *U.S. News & World Report* (December 9, 1985), 52–62.
8. Edgar Allan Poe, "Annabel Lee," in *Yale Book of American Verse*, ed. Thomas R. Lounsbury, 186–187 (New Haven, CT: Yale University, 1912), public domain. http://ia301315.us.archive.org/2/items/yalebookofameric009397mbp/yalebookofameric009397mbp.pdf.
9. John S. Goff, *Robert Todd Lincoln: A Man in His Own Right* (Norman: University of Oklahoma), 70–71.
10. Calvin Miller, *The Finale* (Downer's Grove, IL: InterVarsity, 1979), 21.
11. Attributed to Eleanor Roosevelt.
12. Claudia Wells, "The Multitasking Generation," *Time* (March 29, 2006), 51.
13. Wells, "Multitasking Generation," 50–51.
14. Laurens van der Post and Jane Taylor, *Testament to the Bushmen* (New York: Viking, 1984), 130–31.
15. Thomas J. Peters and Nancy Austin, *A Passion for Excellence* (New York: Random House, 1985), 419.

16. David Ogilvy, *Confessions of an Advertising Man* (New York: Atheneum, 1980), 142.

17. Eugene Peterson, "Success or Failure," *Leadership,* no. 4, (Winter 1984): 53.

18. Charles Kingsley, *Leadership,* no. 6 (Summer 1985): 37.

19. George Bennard, "The Old Rugged Cross," 1913, public domain.

20. For books and DVD studies that develop the grace-based model of family, parenting, and grandparenting, go to www.familymatters.net.

21. One of the best investments of time and money in your marriage is the Weekend to Remember. For the one nearest you, visit www.familylife.com.

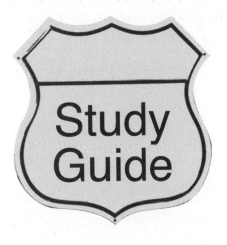

Chapter 1: In Search of Peace and Quiet

Discuss:

1. How would you define *peace*? Do you think you have it? Why or why not?

2. Bill Cosby once said, "The truth is that parents are not really interested in justice. They just want quiet." In his own humorous way, what do you think he was saying? Do you agree? Explain.

3. What area of your life is most likely to rob you of peace? How does it do this?

4. Tim Kimmel writes, "Genuine rest is never far away from the middle of a challenge." What does he mean? If possible, give an example of this from your own life.

5. Tim tells the story of a contest held to illustrate peace. If you were to enter such a contest, what might your picture look like? How would you illustrate peace?

Examine:

1. Read Joshua 1:13.
   A. What promise is given in this verse?
   B. What command is given in this verse?
   C. Where does rest come from according to this verse?

2. Read Psalm 62:1–7.
   A. What do you learn about rest in this passage?
   B. What relationship do verses 1, 2, and 5–7 have to verses 3–4? In what way do you think these verses are meant to "connect" with your own life?
   C. Compare verse 1 with verse 5. What is the same? What is different? What might account for the difference?

Apply:

1. If you were to rank your experience of rest on a scale from 1 (no rest) to 10 (perfect rest), where would you be on the scale? Are you satisfied with this ranking? Explain.

2. Take a few moments to ask God to enable you to see areas in your life in which you need to seek His rest. Then ask Him to give you the strength and wisdom to rest in His rest.

Chapter 2: Seven Marks of a Hurried Family

Discuss:

1. Discuss each of the seven marks of a hurried family. Which characteristics most apply to your own family?

   A. We can't relax; we are restless, not resourceful.

   B. We can't enjoy quiet; we are intimidated by silence.

   C. We never feel satisfied; contentment is always just around the corner.

   D. We lack absolutes; we tend to choose the immediate over the permanent.

   E. We are "suffering servants"; we struggle for approval.

   F. We're like the storm beneath the calm; we are worriers, control freaks.

   G. We are world-class overachievers; we can't stand to lose.

2. Discuss the four common threads of all hurried families:

   ◆ an inability to believe
   ◆ general discontent
   ◆ lack of genuine intimacy
   ◆ a tendency to control

   What part does each of these threads play in creating a home that lacks genuine rest? Do you see any of these four threads in your own home? If so, in what way?

3. Tim writes that sin is "the desire to have it now." Do you agree with him? How can this attitude rob you of rest?

Examine:

1. Read Hebrews 3:7–19. What is the connection in this passage between belief and rest? What promise is given to those who believe?
2. Read Hebrews 13:5–6. Why should we be content with what we have, according to this passage?
3. Read James 4:8. What kind of intimacy does this verse both command and promise?

Apply:

1. Pick the one area of your life in which you most struggle to find rest; then develop a step-by-step plan to address it. At the end of the month, evaluate whether your plan is beginning to work.

Chapter 3: The Foundation for Genuine Rest

Discuss:

1. How does a medical emergency (like that which afflicted Tim's newborn daughter) sometimes help to focus our attention on the issue of rest? Why does it often take such a situation to get our attention?
2. Tim writes that "rest is a choice." What does he mean by this? Do you agree with him? Explain.
3. Tim says all of us have three inner needs:
   - Security: the need for love
   - Significance: the need for purpose
   - Strength: the need for hope

   Which of these three do you feel you have the best grip on? Which of these three do you struggle with the most? Why?

Examine:

1. Read Romans 8:32. In what way does this verse provide a foundation for a lifetime of genuine rest?
2. Read Isaiah 30:15–18.
   A. What foundation is laid in verse 15?
   B. How do God's people sometimes respond to this foundation (v. 16)?
   C. What is the result of responding this way (vv. 16–17)?
   D. What is God's reaction to our response (v. 18)?

Apply:

1. Imagine that a non-Christian has asked you how to find rest in his or her life. Write out a one-page response to this question. Then go back through your response and ask yourself, *Am I living out this answer? Can this person see the results of God's rest in my own life?* Commit this exercise to God, and allow Him to speak to your heart through it.

Chapter 4: A Forgiving Spirit

Discuss:

1. Is it ever hard for you to forgive someone? What kinds of situations are the most difficult for you? How do you usually respond to these situations?
2. Imagine you were a family member of one of the Koreans burned alive inside their church building. Would it have been difficult for you to forgive? Explain.
3. In what way is forgiveness a key to finding rest? What does lack of forgiveness produce in your own life?
4. Why do you think Tim chose forgiveness as the first of his six non-negotiable principles for finding rest? What is so key about this principle?

Examine:
1. Read 1 Peter 2:18–23.
    A. How does this passage relate to forgiveness?
    B. How did Jesus show His forgiveness of those who abused Him?
    C. What does this passage instruct believers to do?
2. Read Ephesians 4:31–32.
    A. What negative commands are we given in this passage? What positive commands? Why are both necessary?
    B. What reason is given for our forgiveness of others?

Apply:
1. Take some unhurried time to read and pray through Luke 7:36–50. Ask God to bring to your mind any lessons you need to learn about forgiveness. Then ask Him to bring to mind anyone you need to ask for forgiveness or anyone who has injured you and stands in need of your forgiveness. Ask for the grace to do whatever you need to.

Chapter 5: Living Within the Limits

Discuss:
1. Why do you think we all have a tendency to want to "walk outside the boundaries"?
2. Think of an instance when someone you knew walked outside of God's boundaries. What happened?
3. How is guilt supposed to function in a Christian's life? Is there such a thing as inappropriate guilt? If so, what is it?
4. What is the difference between beliefs and values?

Examine:
1. Read 2 Corinthians 7:8–10.

A. What action did Paul take with the Corinthians? How did he feel about it?

B. What role did guilt play in this interchange?

C. What does godly guilt always lead to (v. 10)?

2. Read Joshua 1:8. What guidelines are given in this verse for living within God's boundaries? What is promised for those who live within God's boundaries?

Apply:

1. Using paper and pencil, figure out how much time you spent in God's Word:

   ♦ yesterday

   ♦ last week

   ♦ last month

   Are you satisfied with your record? Why or why not? If you want to change your habits, what would you have to do differently? Take a few moments to craft a simple plan that you can implement this week.

Chapter 6: An Eternal Perspective

Discuss:

1. How can you tell if someone's perspective is focused on the now or on the eternal?

2. Tim explains that everyday life must be lived against the backdrop of eternity. What does he mean? Do you agree with him? If so, how is this to be done practically?

3. What does the Hiroshima story teach us about living according to an eternal perspective?

4. Tim says that living according to an eternal perspective changes the way we view love, death, aging, and time. How

does our perspective affect our outlook in each of these areas? How does it affect your own outlook?

5. Tim writes that we should "never sacrifice the permanent on the altar of the immediate." What does this mean? How does someone do that? Give some examples.

Examine:

1. Read Psalm 23. How does this passage view death? How does an eternal perspective change the way we view death?

2. Read 1 Corinthians 15:19. What does Paul say in this verse? What does he mean? Why does he say what he does?

3. Read 2 Corinthians 4:16–18. What does this verse teach about having an eternal perspective? How do you get one? What does it accomplish?

Apply:

1. Take a few unhurried moments to meditate on the following questions. How does an eternal perspective express itself practically in these areas of your life?
   - work life
   - family life
   - social life
   - church life
   - personal life

Chapter 7: Serving While Suffering

Discuss:

1. How does suffering often take away our rest? Does it sometimes do this to you? Explain.

2. Tim explains that accepting and serving are the best antidotes

for suffering. What does he mean? Do you agree with him? Why or why not?

3. Tim says there are four types of people whose rest is obliterated by suffering:

- the bewildered
- the badgered
- the broken
- the battered

In your own words, describe each of these groups. Then identify which of them most closely resembles your own household, and explain why this is so.

Examine:

1. Read Mark 8:34. What does this verse teach us about suffering? How does this relate to peace and rest?
2. Read Matthew 5:43–45. How does Jesus instruct us here to respond to those who hurt us? What reason does He give for such a response?
3. Read Matthew 11:28–30. How does Jesus instruct us to find rest? How does this relate to finding rest in the midst of suffering?
4. Read 1 Peter 4:12–19. According to this text, how should we react to suffering? Why should we react in this way? How are we able to react in this way (v. 19)?

Apply:

1. Look through a concordance at all the verses that refer to suffering. What connection do you see between suffering and rest in these texts? Which texts seem most appropriate for your own situation?
2. Read Richard Wurmbrand's *Tortured for Christ,* and note how

one Christian man responded to suffering—and the results it produced in his life.

Chapter 8: Managing Your Expectations

Discuss:

1. Does *discipline* sound like an appealing term to your ears? Why or why not? What images does it evoke?
2. Tim describes how a lack of discipline leads to feeling incomplete. In what way is this so? Have you ever seen this principle at work in your own life or in the lives of those close to you? If so, describe what you saw.
3. Do you consider yourself a contented person? Explain.
4. How often do you find yourself saying (or thinking), "If only…"? In what context do you usually use this phrase?
5. If you had to write out a single paragraph on the theme "What I Expect Out of Life," what would you say?

Examine:

1. Read Exodus 20:2–3, 17. What is the first commandment? What is the last commandment? Why do you think they're placed where they are? What does this placement say about finding rest and contentment?
2. Read Matthew 6:33. What is God's "formula" for finding contentment? How does this lead to genuine rest? How easy is this for you to experience in your own life?
3. Read 1 Timothy 6:6–10. What is the road to contentment, according to verse 6? What rationale for this does Paul give in verse 7? With what should we be content (v. 8)? What is the problem with rejecting this counsel (vv. 9–10)? How does this passage relate to experiencing rest?

Chapter 9: Managing Your Strengths

Discuss:

1. What are your three greatest strengths? How easy is it for you to name them?
2. How would you define *stewardship*? Comment on Tim's suggested definition of *stewardship*: "The conscientious management of the things that really matter."
3. What are the chief resources you are responsible to manage for the Lord? What guidelines do you employ to manage them effectively?
4. Tim mentions the importance of our calling, our connections, and our capabilities. In your own words, define each of these, and explain how each of them either contributes to or diminishes your own experience of genuine peace.

Examine:

1. Read 1 Corinthians 3:10–15. What does this passage tell us about effective stewardship? What things "really matter" in this passage? What promise is given? What warning is given?
2. Read Psalm 1. How does this psalm teach us to manage our strengths? What regimen does it prescribe? What practices does it warn against?
3. Read Luke 12:35–48. What is the main point of the parable? How does Jesus apply this main point in verse 48? How does this relate to experiencing genuine peace?

Chapter 10: Little House on the Internet

Discuss:

1. List the pros and cons of how your life has changed since you got a cell phone and e-mail.

Pros:

Cons:

What can you do to make your Cons list shorter?

2. Have you ever caught yourself being distracted by the "call of the wireless" during a very important event? What were your choices at that moment? Would you choose the same response now?

3. Is there anything you are allowing into your life that could be sending a mixed message to your children (TV programs, Internet sites, cell phone etiquette)? How could you change in order to use this challenge to model a positive choice?

4. Take an assessment of your "screen" time (TV, computer, phone) versus your "seen" time (face to face). Which takes up more of your pre- and post-office hours? If necessary, how can you change that?

Examine:

1. How does Romans 12:9–12, 21 apply to our challenge to keep technology an asset within our families? What are some practical ways we can do what this passage tells us?

2. Using Philippians 4:8 as your standard for appropriate content and incoming information via technology, how are you doing? What needs to be changed?

3. How can each fruit of the Spirit in Galatians 5:22–23 help you take control of technology and use it for the benefit of your family and God's kingdom?

Apply:

1. Keep your eye out for a news story that tells about a person who used technology for either good or evil. Discuss this

choice with your kids, and let them come to some conclusions about what might have led up to this decision and what the ramifications will be in this person's life and family. (For more topics to discuss with your children, go to Dinner Dialogue at www.familymatters.net)

2. Turn off every piece of technology in your house for one hour. Use that time to interview your spouse and/or your children about their:
   - "dream" day, vacation, job
   - favorite movie, food, book, candy, sport
   - best friend, teacher, lesson

3. Next time your phone interrupts a family moment, resist the urge to answer it. Do this several times, and then calculate how important those calls were compared to what you would have missed.

Chapter 11: Bringing Rest to Your Marriage

Discuss:

1. Why do you think marriage is so frequently a battleground for finding genuine rest?

2. What kinds of attitudes do you think are necessary for enjoying rest in your own marriage?

3. Tim defines love as "the commitment of my will to your needs and best interests regardless of the cost." Do you basically agree with him? Why or why not?

4. Tim writes that love takes self-discipline, sensitivity, and sacrifice. What does each of these mean to you? Which comes most naturally to you? Which presents the biggest struggle?

5. Tim believes that love requires unilateral action and that anything less is not a true demonstration of love. Do you agree? Explain.

Examine:

1. Read 1 Corinthians 13:1–7. Make a list on a sheet of paper with two headings: "Love is" and "Love is not." Then, under the appropriate column, arrange the elements of love Paul named. What can you learn about love from this exercise? How does this relate to peace and rest in the home?

2. Read Ephesians 5:22–33. What principles are given here for enjoying rest in the home? Which principles do you think are the least followed in our culture? Explain.

3. Read 1 Peter 3:1–7. Compare this text with the previous one. How are they similar? How are they different? What do you learn about rest in each of them?

Apply:

1. Take at least thirty minutes to sit down with your spouse and evaluate the "rest quotient" in your marriage. How much rest do the two of you enjoy together? What areas of your marriage make for rest and peace? What areas are challenges for you? What can you do as a couple to experience more of the rest God wants for you?

Chapter 12: Giving the Gift of Rest to Your Children

Discuss:

1. Some would say that *rest* and *children* never go together. How would you respond to such a statement?

2. Tim writes that parenthood is "a temporary responsibility with eternal consequences." How does this make you feel? Does this motivate you in any way? Explain.

3. Tim says that parents have two priorities in rearing their kids in a godly home: preparation and protection. Which area do

you have the better handle on? In which area would you most like help? Explain.

4. There are four primary spheres of development a parent must address in rearing children:
   - physical
   - emotional
   - intellectual
   - spiritual

   Which of these is the greatest challenge for you? Brainstorm how you might find the help you need in this area. Then try at least one of these new approaches and evaluate how it works.

Examine:

1. Read Ephesians 6:4 and Colossians 3:21.
   A. What advice do these texts give to Christian parents? How is this advice connected to peace in the home?
   B. Read Luke 2:51–52. In what areas did Jesus develop as a boy, according to this text? How can this give Christian parents hope for their own families?
2. Read Deuteronomy 6:4–9. What commands are given to faithful parents in the raising of their families? What practical instruction is offered? How would following this instruction result in a more restful home?

Apply:

1. Take part of an evening to sit down with your spouse and evaluate the support you are giving your children in each of the four areas Tim talks about: physical, emotional, intellectual, spiritual. Celebrate the victories, and plan a strategy for improving any weak areas. Then spend several minutes thanking God for the privilege of rearing children, asking

Him to give you wisdom in bringing all your children to a healthy fear of the Lord.

Chapter 13: Maintaining Rest in the Work Arena

Discuss:

1. How would you define *success*? How would your peers at work describe it? What tension (if any) exists between these two viewpoints?

2. Why does Tim teach that inner needs cannot be satisfied with things? If this is true, then why do so many of us spend so much time chasing after things?

3. Why is courage necessary for maintaining rest in the work arena?

4. Why should the world's idea of success never be pursued as a goal? To what does it lead?

5. What level of satisfaction have you adopted in the following areas:
   - house
   - job
   - neighborhood
   - church
   - recreational opportunities

6. Do you live by any rules of good stewardship? If so, what are they? If not, why not?

7. Tim writes that we will either sacrifice now or forever. What does he mean? Do you agree with him? Explain.

Examine:

1. Read Genesis 2:1–3 and Exodus 20:8–11. What commands about work are given here? What reasoning for these commands

is offered? How do these commands relate to enjoying genuine rest?

2. Read Luke 10:38–42. Who experienced God's rest in this
   story? Why? Who didn't? Why? What lesson can you draw
   from this story?

3. Read 1 Corinthians 15:58. What command is given in this
   passage? How can you derive rest from what is said here?

Chapter 14: Gaining Rest
in Your Relationships

Discuss:

1. Complete the following sentence: "I know I can always count
   on my friends to _____."

2. Is involvement at church a regular part of your lifestyle? Why
   or why not?

3. Tim says good friendships are based on loyalty, honesty, and
   sensitivity. Which of these elements is most important to
   you? Why?

4. Tim says a good church is focused on the Lord, on the Scriptures, and on families. Would you have picked these same
   three elements? Why or why not?

5. Do your own relationships seem to help you experience
   God's rest? Explain.

Examine:

1. Read Proverbs 27:6. What kind of wounds is this text talking
   about? What does it mean by "kisses"? In what way can
   wounds even be better than kisses?

2. Read Hebrews 10:24–25. What do these verses have to say
   about our involvement at church? Why does the writer insist
   that we be active at church? What benefits accrue?

3. Read Jeremiah 29:13. Who finds God, according to this text? How is this the ultimate key to finding rest? Compare this to Isaiah 57:21. How do these verses contrast? How can one get from "no peace" to peace?

Apply:

1. Make it a point this week to tell your closest two friends how much they mean to you and why. Be specific in what you most appreciate about them.

2. Spend some time in the next few days thinking through your involvement at church and its ministry to you. Then consider setting up a lunch date with your pastor to talk over your conclusions, both positive and negative.

Now that you have read Tim Kimmel's life-changing book, *Little House on the Freeway*, you may be asking, "Where do I go from here?"

Want More?

The Hurried Family Video Study is the perfect way for you to apply these revolutionary principles to your daily life. Why not spend the next few weeks going through this fun, interactive small group study with friends or neighbors? You'll have a blast and get the support you need as you discuss the ideas in this book with people who care.

Don't miss *The Hurried Family Video Study*. It will empower you and your family with practical, stress saving skills as you take the off-ramp to sanity, peace and family harmony.

Kit includes:

* Eight 15-20 minute sessions on 2 DVD's

* Eight Participant Workbooks (additional workbooks are available)

* One copy of the book, *Little House On The Freeway*

* One Facilitator CD-ROM
  • Facilitator Guide (PDF)
  • Promotional Materials

In this age of stress and crazy schedules, you can never have enough help and hope in the middle of the hurry. Don't miss out, call or go online today to order *The Hurried Family Video Study*.

www.HurriedFamily.com
800.467.4596

building grace-based relationships

www.FamilyMatters.net

Family Matters® creates resources and conducts conferences across the country on the unique pressures that confront today's families.

Dr. Tim Kimmel and his wife Darcy are the founders of Family Matters®, a non-profit ministry whose goal is to see families transformed by God into instruments of restoration and reformation. At Family Matters® we believe families are the foundation of a successful and strong society. Our ministry philosophy embraces a grace-based approach to relationships, provides a solid grasp of the "big picture" of parenting, promotes a character-driven strategy for parenting, and shows family members how to leave a legacy that never dies.

FamilyMatters.net

For more information about our books, video studies, conferences and other tools that equip and encourage families for every age and stage of life, please visit us at FamilyMatters.net.